SO YOU THINK YOU'RE A

New Testament writer

Text copyright © Mike Coles 2004
The author asserts the moral right
to be identified as the author of this work

Published by
The Bible Reading Fellowship
First Floor, Elsfield Hall
15–17 Elsfield Way, Oxford OX2 8FG

ISBN 1 84101 183 5
First published 2004
1 3 5 7 9 10 8 6 4 2 0
All rights reserved

Acknowledgments
Scripture quotations taken from The New Revised Standard Version of the
Bible, Anglicized Edition, are copyright © 1989, 1995 by the Division of
Christian Education of the National Council of the Churches of Christ in the
USA, and are used by permission. All rights reserved.

Scripture quotations taken from the Holy Bible, New International Version,
copyright © 1973, 1978, 1984 by International Bible Society, are used by
permission of Hodder & Stoughton Limited. All rights reserved.
'NIV' is a registered trademark of International Bible Society.
UK trademark number 1448790.

Scriptures quoted from the Good News Bible published by The Bible
Societies/HarperCollins Publishers Ltd, UK © American Bible Society 1966,
1971, 1976, 1992, used with permission.

Scripture quotations taken from the Contemporary English Version of the
Bible published by HarperCollins Publishers are copyright © 1991, 1992,
1995 American Bible Society.

A catalogue record for this book is available from the British Library

Printed and bound in Great Britain by Bookmarque, Croydon

SO YOU THINK YOU'RE A

New Testament writer

MIKE COLES

In loving memory of my dear Dad,
who died in December 2003.
He was such a lovely man,
and the best Dad anyone could have.
May he rest in peace and rise in glory.

Contents

INTRODUCTION

Before the show begins, there are a few points that you will need to bear in mind.

First, the show is actually 'outside time'. In other words, there is no exact time when the show takes place. All you need to know is that it is some time during the first century AD. The actual date is not important. Each show begins in the late afternoon / early evening.

Second, the venue. Here, you need to imagine the show taking place at the home of a wealthy person living in Jerusalem. The house has a huge courtyard, with two or three rooms built around. The large courtyard is set up with a small stage at one end, and stools and backed chairs facing it for the audience.

Finally, when the Bible is quoted, no one translation is ever used. It will often depend on who is quoting the text and what style is appropriate. And so, straight on to the show.

Standing in the middle of the stage, Mike begins:

MIKE: Hi there, folks. Welcome to this brand new and exciting show. What a great honour it is for me to be able to chat to some of the chaps who were responsible for writing those books that make up the New Testament. That's right, folks, those 27 wonderful books!

Now, we all know that there would be no books, no New Testament and no show here tonight if it had not been for that most remarkable man, Jesus. Jesus didn't leave us any writings, but we know that his life and ministry, and what he said it all meant, were preserved and passed on by some of his main followers. Despite absolutely awful persecution, these followers spread the message far and wide. Their message was simple: God had become human in Jesus Christ. This Jesus came to show us all what God is like, how he would save us, and how we should live.

My special guests, the New Testament writers, show Jesus as the person who fulfils centuries of promise and hope, of wonderful prophecies that echo throughout the Old Testament. My guests also write about how Jesus will return a second time to establish a kingdom of love, justice and truth. They tell us that Jesus invites us to say sorry for all our sins, to turn to God, to accept that Jesus died on the cross to wipe away all our sins, and that we should make Jesus central in our lives and ask him to help us in our everyday lives to please God.

Well, folks, what a powerful message this New Testament contains. I am delighted to say that over the next five weeks, I will have the honour and pleasure to speak to... wait for it... Matthew, Mark, Luke, John and last, but by no means least, Paul!

Mike Coles chats to Matthew

MUSICAL INTRODUCTION

Just before the show proper begins, a small group of musicians walk on to the stage. They are mainly singers, male and female, but some of them play rhythm and melody instruments. You'll hear more about music during biblical times later in the show.

The group begin the show by singing the words of Mary in that amazing song of praise recorded in Luke, chapter 1, verses 46 to 55.

These words were used as a great hymn in worship at a very early date. The audience also join in, as most of them know the words, and they make a glorious sound.

At the end the audience applaud and cheer. The music group exit the stage. Mike thanks the group as they leave.

MIKE: Now, ladies and gentlemen, without any further ado, I would like you to welcome this week's guest, that one-time dodgy tax collector turned good—Matthew, son of Alphaeus!

The audience give Matthew a warm welcome, with plenty of enthusiastic applause, although there are one or two heckles, and a few 'boos' can be heard.

MIKE: Matthew, welcome to this brand new show. I'm sorry about the hecklers. There are obviously a few folk in the audience who still remember you as a tax collector!

MATTHEW: God bless you, Mike. It's great to be here. Don't worry about the hecklers. I can totally understand their anger. In fact, I do remember one or two of their faces from back in Capernaum, where I was a greedy man. I hope that later in the show I'll get a chance to explain myself and apologize for my pretty awful past.

MIKE: Most definitely, Matthew. In fact, I look forward to chatting about your tax collecting days a little later.

You know, I have to say, you really are looking remarkably well. What's your secret?

MATTHEW: Plenty of olives and olive oil, Mike. That's the secret—and fish when I can afford it!

MIKE: Sounds like great advice to me!

So, Matthew, tell me a little about your upbringing. You're quite an educated chap, aren't you?

MATTHEW: My dad was a strict man. He made sure I became fluent in both Aramaic and Greek, and from a young age I was quite skilled in arithmetic.

Someone shouts from the audience, 'You can't have been that good at maths, mate! You used to charge me far too much as a bloomin' tax collector!'

MIKE: Oh dear, we're back on that again. OK, then, let's talk about those days. Why tax collecting?

MATTHEW: It was simply for the cash, Mike. I was greedy. The Roman government saw me as an educated man, skilled in maths. They told me I'd make a fair bit of money, and I did.

MIKE: Matthew, tell us why tax collectors are so hated. Try to explain why you've got a few enemies in the audience tonight.

MATTHEW: Well, obviously, nobody likes to pay taxes at the best of times. But there are three reasons why we're so unpopular.

First, the Romans employed us, and they're hated by the Jews because they're occupying our land. I'm Jewish myself, of course, so my fellow countrymen thought I was a traitor for working for the Romans.

Second, we have a reputation for being dishonest. The Romans let us charge a rate of tax that would also provide a living for ourselves. Some of us, including me, interpreted this privilege more liberally than others.

Finally, as tax collectors, we often come into contact with Gentiles (that means anyone who's not Jewish), which according to the Jewish faith makes us 'unclean'.

But of course, that's all in the past. I am so sorry to all those I cheated. Those of you in the audience whom I've offended, I beg your forgiveness. Since meeting Jesus, my whole life has changed. I was a wicked man, and I am really sorry.

At this point there is a huge round of applause from the audience.

MIKE: Thanks for being so honest. You've certainly won all the audience over now. This brings us on nicely to one of the biggest questions I wanted to ask you this evening. We've talked a little about your past, but what we're all dying to know is, what happened? One minute you're a lousy tax collector, making money, partying every other night, making all sorts of enemies, and the next minute you give all this up. Your whole life just turned upside down. Matthew, could you please tell us how this man Jesus changed your life?

MATTHEW: As a tax collector on the big toll road running through Capernaum, I used to get to hear about everything that was going on in the area. I started to hear about this man called Jesus. People were describing him as a rabbi with a real difference. I heard folk saying that he had performed miracles, healing folk all over the place. I'd heard that he was a wonderful storyteller. People were saying that he wasn't like the other Jewish teachers they knew. He didn't walk around thinking he was all it, trying to look really holy and important like some religious teachers and leaders I've come across!

The other thing that really interested me was that I'd heard that he mixed with anyone and everyone; apparently, he didn't go around telling people how wicked they were. As a tax collector I was criticized almost every day by the other Jewish leaders and teachers of the Law. To hear about a teacher who didn't try to make people feel guilty fascinated me. I began to look forward to coming across this Jesus from Nazareth.

The other thing I would like to say is that, during this stage in my life, I wasn't really happy. Yes, I had money, I threw parties every other night, but I wasn't happy. Who can be totally happy when they're hated by nearly everyone around? The only friends I did have were people like me, fellow tax collectors and other dodgy people.

That's why this chap Jesus really interested me. If he turned up one day while I was collecting taxes, what would he say to me? Would he just condemn me like all the other teachers that used to walk by? I began to think about this a lot.

MIKE: I notice in your Gospel, chapter 9 verse 9, your first meeting with Jesus is described. It's in Mark's Gospel as well, chapter 2 verses 13 and 14, and Luke chapter 5 verses 27 and 28. These Gospel accounts say what happened, but not what was going through your mind. Tell us about it.

MATTHEW: Like I mentioned before, Mike, I was not a happy chap, and I had been hearing a great deal about this man Jesus, the rabbi. Deep down, I really was hoping that I might get the chance to meet him. I'd heard how he had changed people's lives, and that's what I wanted—some sort of change in my life. Exactly what change, I didn't know. But things were not right.

It was one afternoon in Capernaum when I heard a large crowd walking towards me. I began to hear people shouting out the name of Jesus. I can tell you now, my heart starting beating like the clappers. This was the man I had heard so much about, and before I knew it, he was standing in front of me. He stared at me. I expected to get a load of abuse as per usual—to be told what a terrible sinner I was. Instead, I heard the two most amazing words I'd ever heard, two words that were to change my entire life. Jesus simply said to me, 'Follow me.'

Well, Mike, you can only imagine my reaction. At that precise moment, my life was turned upside down. A rabbi had spoken to me kindly, not judged me as a sinner. But not only that, I was being given the opportunity to follow him—this great man, the talk of the town. I had tears in my eyes; a great weight was lifted from my heart. I knew at that moment, I couldn't spend another second collecting taxes. I was aware that if you gave up your rights as a tax collector, you could never go back to the job, but I didn't care. Jesus had called me.

At this point there is a huge round of applause from the audience. Many members of the audience are clearly moved after listening to Matthew's words.

MIKE: It's a real pleasure to have you share that experience with us, Matthew. Did you literally just drop everything and follow Jesus?

MATTHEW: That's exactly what I did! I wanted to start everything again, there and then. I was just rotting away inside. Jesus saying 'Follow me' was all I needed. There was nothing to hold me back. The money, the partying, all of that just made me more and more miserable. This man Jesus, and what he had to offer, was all I wanted.

MIKE: Many folk already thought that Jesus was crazy asking you, a dodgy tax collector, to join him. Didn't he then go on to your house later that evening and mix with a whole load of down-and-out 'sinners'?

MATTHEW: He certainly did. Once I'd walked out of my office, I immediately asked Jesus if he'd like to have supper with me that evening. I did it as a little gesture of hospitality.

I was a tax collector, and Jesus still spoke to me and cared for me, so I also invited loads of other tax collectors along, and all sorts of 'sinners'—mainly what you might call non-observant Jews, the ones who didn't follow the teachings of the Law.

We had a great evening! Many of my guests were really moved that Jesus, this great rabbi, dared enter a house full of so many disreputable people. I can tell you now, it wasn't just my life that changed that day, but many of my guests thought very deeply about their own lives after listening to Jesus talk and teach.

MIKE: You mention in your Gospel that during this meal some Pharisees turned up and started moaning about Jesus. Who were these people and what actually happened?

MATTHEW: The Pharisees were the teachers who were really keen on keeping all the tiniest details of the Law, so I think you can all probably guess why they weren't happy. They simply asked Jesus' disciples why Jesus, the rabbi, was mixing with all these sinners. How could Jesus, if he was in his right mind, eat with us lot? Jesus heard what they were saying, and what he went on to say in reply was wonderful.

MIKE: That's right. Didn't he say something about needing a doctor and being sick?

MATTHEW: What he said, Mike, was brilliant, as it always was! He said to the Pharisees, 'People who are well do not need a doctor, only those who are sick.' The great thing then was that he gave them some homework to do.

The audience laugh.

MATTHEW: He said to them, 'Go and find out what is meant by the scripture that says: "It's kindness that I want, not animal sacrifices." I haven't come to call respectable people, but all the outcasts.'

MIKE: Excellent stuff! I presume that Jesus was making the point that what really counts is human relationships, not just religious rule-keeping.

MATTHEW: Yes, what we see here is Jesus expressing his compassion for sinners. That's why he came, that was his mission—to save sinners. Jesus was also having a go at the self-righteousness of the Pharisees. They weren't all bad, but many of them walked around so full of themselves. They didn't realize that they too were sick and needed a doctor.

Big cheers from the audience.

MIKE: I think most of tonight's audience have come across some of these dodgy Pharisees from time to time!

At this point in the show, Matthew (and I hope you don't mind), I'd like to go over to the audience and ask them if they've got any questions for you.

MATTHEW: I'd be delighted to answer any questions, Mike, as long as they're not too tricky!

Audience laugh.

MIKE: So, ladies and gentlemen, boys and girls, who would like to start the ball rolling?

OK, the lady in the third row, wearing the blue tunic with the embroidered edges around the neckline.[1] Yes, you're the one. Could you tell us your name, where you're from, and what's your question?

'Good evening. My name is Rebekah from Caesarea Philippi. First of all, I'd like to say how excited I am to be here tonight. God bless you, Matthew. Could you please explain why it is that, in your Gospel, you quote from the Old Testament 41 times, which is a great deal more than the other Gospel writers?'

MATTHEW: Well, good evening, Rebekah. I'm just as excited as you about being here, and may God bless you too! Thanks for the great question—was it really 41 times? My immediate answer to you is to point out where my Gospel has been placed in the Bible. It follows immediately after the Old Testament, and stands at the beginning of the New. In other words, it's like a link between the two. One of the main reasons why I wrote my Gospel was to show that Jesus is the Messiah—the great leader promised in the Old Testament. You may all have noticed that in the 41 times I quote from the Old Testament, I nearly always say, '... so that it might be fulfilled'.

Also, to answer the question, I need to remind you that in the first place I wrote my Gospel for Jewish Christians, to help strengthen their faith that Jesus truly is the Messiah. The 41 times I quote from the Old Testament are to show that Jesus is the fulfilment of all Old Testament prophecy. Christ was not only born as a Jew, but he was also sent, first, to the Jews. As the prophet Isaiah said (Oops! Here I go again), 'Unto us a child is born, unto us a son is given.'

A big round of applause from the audience.

MIKE: A great question, Rebekah! Thanks for that, and thank you, Matthew, for that very interesting answer. I think we'll take one more question from the audience, and then we'll have a little break and listen to some great music. More about that in a moment. Now, would anyone else like to ask Matthew a question?

OK, the man at the back who has just arrived with his mule—the one that has just made a big mess on our floor, but never mind. Yes, you, sir. What's your name, where are you from, and what's your question for Matthew?

'Good evening, Mike, and good evening, Matthew. Sorry about the animal; he's not been feeling himself recently. My name is Joshua, from Bethlehem. Matthew, it's great to be here this evening listening to you. Could you tell me a little about Jesus' "Sermon on the Mount", as we all like to call it today? We know that Moses gave the Ten Commandments to the Israelites

years ago. Is Jesus to be seen as the "new Moses", giving his commandments to the people?'

MATTHEW: Good evening, Joshua. Thank you for your kind words, and I do hope your mule feels better soon. In fact, I think we all do! So, you're from Bethlehem. Can I repeat the Old Testament quote that I used in chapter 2 verse 6 of my Gospel?

'Yes!' the whole audience shout.

MATTHEW: 'Bethlehem Ephrathah, you may be one of the smallest towns in Judah, but from you I will bring a ruler who will guide my people Israel.' That, of course, was Micah's prophecy about the birth of our Messiah.

So, the 'Sermon on the Mount'. You are quite right, Joshua. My aim is to show Jesus as the new Moses giving the new law to the new Israel on a new mountain. We Jews always expected our Messiah to fulfil the law of Moses, or to give the law some sort of deeper meaning. That's why I quote Jesus in chapter 5 verse 17, when he says, 'Do not think that I have come here to get rid of the Law or the Prophets; I haven't come to abolish them but to fulfil them.' I'm trying to show Jesus as the great teacher, teaching with real credibility about the true meaning of the Old Testament law. To many people, the law was simply something written on stone—hundreds of rules to obey. But Jesus brought the law alive; instead of laws written on stone, the law is now written in our hearts. It has been fulfilled— brought to life in our own experience.

Jesus' great sermon is not a collection of laws, because, let's face it, some of the ideals he sets out are virtually impossible to keep. The sermon simply teaches us ways to behave which we should be able to apply to any situation.

MIKE: Matthew, you mention that some of the ideals Jesus teaches are virtually impossible to keep. Do any examples spring to mind?

At this moment, Matthew quickly leans over, and lightly slaps Mike on his right cheek. Mike is a little shocked, as are many of the audience.

MIKE: Good grief, Matthew! I certainly wasn't expecting that. I presume you're going to make a point.

MATTHEW: Indeed I am, Mike. Could I now please slap you on the other cheek?

MIKE: You must be joking!

Audience laugh.

MATTHEW: Listen to the words of Jesus that I recorded in my Gospel, chapter 5 verses 38 and 39.
  'You know how the Law said, "An eye for an eye, and a tooth for a tooth." But now I tell you this: do not take revenge on someone who does wrong to you. If anyone slaps you on the right cheek, let him slap your left cheek too.'

MIKE: Wow! Powerful stuff. I see what you mean about Jesus teaching ideals that are pretty impossible to keep. You know, if I hadn't known you, and you just slapped me on the cheek like you did, I'd have given you a good slap back!

The audience are still laughing.

MATTHEW: Those of us who follow Jesus have to be peacemakers, and we are not to return evil for evil. We are to absorb it and change it into love. Jesus actually went on to say, 'You must be perfect, just as your Father in heaven is perfect.' Jesus didn't come to give us rules—he showed us perfection. We can never be perfect, but we can try. Constantly trying—talking to God in prayer, getting support from other followers and help from the Spirit of Jesus himself—that's what it's all about!

'Amen to that!' shout out many of the audience.

MIKE: Great stuff! If we have time, we may talk about this amazing sermon in a little more detail later. But now, as promised, we have some great entertainment for you. This evening's music will be performed by that wonderful group of musicians, Zebedee and his Magic Singers and Harps! They'll be singing Psalm 23 and Psalm 60 for us. A big, warm welcome to the band!

The audience cheer, clap and whistle as the band arrives.

While they're playing, it might be worth telling you a little about the band, what instruments they use and so on. Musicians at the time of the New Testament were very important. Music was a vital part of religious life.

Some of the instruments Zebedee's group play are the Hazora, a trumpet made of silver or bronze. The sound it makes is quite sharp. Some members of the band also play the Kinnor, a stringed instrument shaped like a harp. Then there is the Menanaim, a percussion instrument made of metal plates that make a sound when moved. Finally, some of the band play the Tof, another percussion instrument that has a membrane like a drum. There were different sizes of drum, which could be played with the hands or with sticks.

Hebrew music at this time was more concerned with rhythm than melody. There weren't actually very many melodies around, and those that did exist were very popular. Many were folk songs, and they were used to sing some of the Psalms. (For example, Psalm 60 was set to the tune 'Shushan Eduth', which means 'The Lily of Testimony'.)

Well, the music is almost over, and so we go back to the show.

As the band finish Psalm 60, there is a huge round of applause.

MIKE: Fantastic! Thank you so much, Zebedee and the band.

MATTHEW: They were excellent!

MIKE: Matthew, so far this evening, we've heard how you describe Jesus as the person who fulfils all Old Testament prophecy and the

Law. In writing your Gospel, you have made it clear that Jesus in his life and death has, in a way, made Judaism complete. Certainly, compared to the other Gospels, you really do emphasize the importance of Jewish teaching and the Law of Moses. In the light of all this, what would you say to those who might think you're suggesting that the good news is only for Jewish people?

MATTHEW: I would say to them, absolutely not! The good news (which, of course, is what the word 'gospel' actually means) may have grown out of what God did in the Old Testament, but this good news is for the whole world, and that means it's for Jews and Gentiles. In my Gospel, I make this point very clearly. In chapter 8 verses 5 to 13, I recall the story of Jesus healing a Roman officer's servant. Jesus was amazed by that man's faith. He was a Gentile, who would not have had any training in the Jewish scriptures, and yet he recognized Jesus as the Messiah.

I have also recalled Jesus' parable of the tenants in the vineyard, in chapter 21 verses 33 to 46. In that story, after the tenants had killed the owner's son, Jesus said that the owner would kill those evil men, 'and let the vineyard out to other tenants'. Jesus then quoted from Psalm 118 and said, 'The stone which the builders rejected as worthless turned out to be the most important of all. This was done by the Lord; what a wonderful sight it is.'

All of this clearly refers to the fact that Gentiles could be accepted into the Church—the worldwide group of Jesus' followers. Last but not least, Mike, are the words I use to end my Gospel, when Jesus says to his disciples, 'Go now to all peoples everywhere and make them my disciples. Baptize them in the name of the Father, the Son, and the Holy Spirit. Teach them all to obey everything that I have commanded you. I will be with you always, to the end of the age.'

'Alleluia! Alleluia!' shout most of the audience.

MIKE: Thanks, Matthew. Now, I have a letter here sent in by a viewer. Her name is Deborah, and she lives in Capernaum. We need to go back to the Sermon on the Mount again. She would like you to explain Jesus' words in chapter 5 verses 3 to 10, which are the 'Happy are they…' sayings. Deborah is really quite confused about these sayings. For example, she writes, 'How on earth can anyone be happy who is in mourning? How can you be happy if you're poor and down and out? Maybe I'm missing something here, but I really would love it if Matthew could shed some light on these sayings of Jesus.'

Well, Matthew, quite a tough one if you ask me. I'm glad you're answering it and not me.

MATTHEW: Well, thanks very much, Mike! Deborah, thank you very much for your letter. I will do my very best to try to explain the real meaning and beauty of these sayings. If it's OK with you, Mike, could I just recite the sayings first, before explaining them?

MIKE: To think you were actually there, Matthew, when Jesus spoke these words is amazing. We would all love to hear you recite these 'Happiness' sayings of Jesus, wouldn't we, folks?

'Yeah!' shout the whole audience.

MATTHEW: 'Happy are all those folk who know they are spiritually poor, because the kingdom of heaven belongs to them.

'Happy are those people who mourn; God will comfort and help them.

'Happy are those people who are humble; they will receive all that God has promised.

'Happy are those who really hunger and thirst to do what God requires; God will totally satisfy them.

'Happy are those who can show mercy to others; God will be merciful to them.

'Happy are those who are pure in heart; they will truly see God.

'Happy are those who work for peace; they will be God's children.

'Happy are those who are persecuted because they do God's work; the kingdom of heaven belongs to them.'

Many of the audience are moved to tears when they hear these beautiful words of Jesus. There is also some applause.

MATTHEW: If I could just begin by explaining that many folk call these sayings 'the Beatitudes'. The sayings start 'Blessed are…' or 'Happy are…' and Beatitude comes from the Latin word *beatus*, which means 'blessed'.

MIKE: Well, strike a light! I never knew that. What do you think Jesus actually meant when he used this word 'blessed'?

MATTHEW: It's a really powerful word, Mike. This 'blessedness' that Jesus spoke about was a type of deep inner happiness that nothing will ever be able to touch. If you were to ask the average person in the street what would make them happy, they might say, 'more money', or 'a nice house', or even having a healthy mule!

Matthew looks at the chap at the back. Audience laugh. Joshua gives a little wave.

But Jesus turns upside down the average person's idea of happiness. The happiness Jesus speaks of in these sayings is the most wonderful thing any of us could ever experience.

I'd like to explain just briefly the true meaning of each saying now, to try to help Deborah truly understand what it was that Jesus was saying.

The first saying, about those who are spiritually poor, means, quite simply, that until someone realizes they need God, God cannot help them. It's a bit like saying that a doctor can only help someone who knows that they are ill and wants to be cured. It's exactly the same if you want a relationship with God. You can turn your back on God, but if you let God know that you need him, he will be there for you, and you will know true happiness.

MIKE: But next comes the Beatitude that really troubled Deborah— the one about mourning. What's that one all about, Matthew?

MATTHEW: The immediate response, Mike, is to think, 'How on earth can I feel true happiness when I am mourning, when my heart is in pieces?' We all know that grief is always a terrible thing, but in fact we can learn a great deal when we have had experiences Whenever we want really good advice about something, it's always best to turn to people who have been through similar circumstances; they always share real wisdom. If we are truly to grow as human beings, we need to experience suffering in our lives. When we look at it like this, Jesus' saying means exactly what it says. We should also remember that going through awful times can be a great blessing, as then we turn to God for help, and he gives us the greatest help and comfort of all, and helps to put joy back into our hearts.

MIKE: I once heard someone say, 'Storms make a strong tree; testings make a strong Christian!'

MATTHEW: Beautifully put!

MIKE: I must admit, Matthew, that that saying about 'happy are they who mourn' did confuse me a little, but the way you've explained it was wonderful. I really hope Deborah and all of you watching found that as inspiring as I did.

Big round of applause at this point.

MATTHEW: Could I just quickly zoom through the other sayings and their meanings? Of course, the next saying refers to people who are 'humble' or 'meek'. I remember the promise given to the humble in Psalm 37 verse 11: 'the humble will possess the land and enjoy prosperity and peace'.

Humble people, who know their needs rather than boasting about how they can cope all alone, are the spiritually strong ones.

'Happy are those who hunger and thirst to do what God requires,' Jesus said. Quite simply, folks, Jesus was making the point that people who are desperately hungry and thirsty for righteousness, and who want to be close to God, will be totally satisfied. God will fill their hearts with a joy they've never experienced before.

'Happy are those who can show mercy to others.' Mike, I hope you can forgive me for the slap in the face earlier!

MIKE: Why, of course!

MATTHEW: Remember, folks, if we expect God to forgive us (and we can be pretty bad sometimes), then we have to forgive other people. It can be tough to do this sometimes, but we must try, and with God's help we can learn to forgive others even in really difficult situations.

'Happy are the pure in heart.' When Jesus spoke these words, he was talking about our motives. Purity does not come from performing loads of rituals, or from not eating certain types of food. It's all about motives. Many of us may behave generously or kindly, but what are our motives for doing this? To make sure other people see us doing the right thing? I think if we are all honest with ourselves, Mike, there aren't many of us who could say that our motives are always pure. Those that are pure in heart will see God face to face.

This reminds me of a passage in 2 Esdras 7 verse 98: 'The greatest joy of all will be the confident and exultant assurance which will be theirs, free from all fear and shame, as they press forward to see face to face the One whom they served in their lifetime and from whom they are now to receive their reward in glory.'[2]

We're almost at the end now. 'Happy are the peacemakers,' Jesus said. This is not just about people who are non-violent, it's about those who have truly found peace with God and try to share and pass this peace on to others.[3]

Finally, while I was writing my Gospel, the Church was suffering terrible persecution, and many Christians were facing death. Jesus said that this would happen, and this gives us great encouragement. The more the Christians were persecuted, the more Christianity flourished.[4]

MIKE: Matthew, thanks very much for that. You know, I heard some-one the other day refer to these sayings as the 'Be happy attitudes', which I thought was very clever.

'I heard someone call them the "Beautiful attitudes",' shouts someone from the audience.

MATTHEW: I think they're both wonderful ways to describe these sayings of Jesus.

MIKE: OK. It's that time of the show when we have a quick advert. Back in a moment for more fascinating conversation with Matthew.

Two men walk across the stage carrying a large piece of fairly smooth wood. On it are painted the words:

BEST CAST NETS IN ISRAEL!

A third man then appears and says, 'Yes, ladies and gentlemen, my name is David, and I know that many of you here this evening are involved with fishing in one way or another. If you're fed up with your old nets, then look no further. My cast nets are the best you'll find. They're bigger than ever and superbly weighted all around. I'll be here after the show this evening should you wish to come and haggle a price. You won't get a better deal anywhere!'[5]

MIKE: Thanks very much, David. In fact, that reminds me, Matthew—didn't you write in your Gospel that Jesus told a parable about one of these cast nets?

MATTHEW: Well remembered, Mike. It was in chapter 13 verses 47 to 50. Jesus was telling us about God's kingdom and how God was going to judge us all. He described how some fishermen threw out their net in the lake and how they caught all kinds of fish. When the net was full, they pulled it to shore and sat down to divide up all the fish. All the good fish were put in their buckets, and the rubbish, useless fish were thrown away.[6] Of course, the point he was making is that, at the end of time, the angels will separate out all the evil people from the good, and the evil ones will be thrown into the fire.

MIKE: Always makes me shiver a little, Matthew, when I hear about that Day of Judgment.

MATTHEW: Nothing to fear, Mike. Just keep your faith in God; try to be faithful. Remember our chat about the Beatitudes? Just try to follow those teachings, and you will most certainly be seen as someone who is righteous in God's eyes.

MIKE: Well, that's all we can do. Thanks for that, Matthew. Now, we have another letter here, but sadly there is no name with this one. But this is a great question for you. 'Matthew, can you tell us a little about the other disciples, and what it was like suddenly being in a group of twelve totally different people?' That's the question our anonymous letter writer would like to ask you, and to be honest, I think all of us here would love to hear you answer it.

MATTHEW: My, my, now there's a tricky one! It's interesting, actually, because only last week someone asked me why Jesus bothered having any disciples. If you read about us in the Gospels, we do come across as being quite thick. We never seem to understand what Jesus is talking about!

Audience laugh.

It's true, we didn't understand many of Jesus' parables, or miracles, or many of his sayings. But the whole point is that we were just twelve ordinary men—pretty dodgy people before we met Jesus. We were chosen to be disciples, which, as most of you know, means 'pupils—people who learn'. Jesus chose us for a reason. Mark mentions it in his Gospel, when he quotes Jesus saying, 'I've chosen

25

...me. I'm going to send you out to preach and drive
... OK, we may appear to have been a little dopey at
... were there to learn. Jesus was training us to do his

...'m sure any one of us here this evening would have been the same. Actually to be with Jesus, the Son of God, for those few years must have been overwhelming. Us lot, just ordinary folk, and Jesus the Son of God; I mean, how would any of us have coped with being a disciple of Jesus?

Matthew, how did the twelve of you all get on at first? Did you become best mates really quickly, or was it pretty tough?

MATTHEW: You have to remember, Mike, that this whole experience for the twelve of us was just so fantastic and overwhelming. One minute, most of us had regular jobs and ordinary lives, and the next minute we were asked to become disciples of the Son of God. I don't remember having much time to analyse each person. All of us had had some life-changing experience in deciding to follow Jesus, so at one level, we were totally united as his followers.

But to be honest, Mike, at the more human level, I'm sure we did all have some doubts about each other at first. I mean, for a start, I had been a lousy tax collector for years. I'm sure many of the disciples must have wondered how Jesus could have asked me to follow him. I remember Peter making a bit of a fuss about me joining the team. I could quite understand that because, as a tax collector, I used to really clobber fishermen, especially when I'd heard there had been a good catch. Peter certainly gave me a few funny looks at first!

Some of us also wondered about Simon the ex-Zealot[8] being part of the team. I mean, this man had probably killed quite a few Romans. He must certainly have hated tax collectors more than anyone, as we worked for the Romans. What must he have thought of me? I did wonder at first whether he was going to sneak up to me one evening and slit my throat.

I could go on and on talking about the suspicions and diffic
we may have had in the early days. But we came to realize in quite
short time that we had all come with a past. And this didn't matter.
Jesus was transforming our lives. We learned to love and to forgive,
and to work together. For the first time ever, I was no longer greedy.
I began to discover what it meant to be truly rich. Simon the ex-
Zealot once thought that only through force and violence could anyone change things. He came to understand that love and forgiveness
were a far more powerful force, and that it was only love that could
truly transform lives. We all came to learn this.

MIKE: Well, you've certainly answered part of the anonymous letter
we received. The other part of the letter wanted you to tell us a little
about the other disciples. Sadly, we don't really have time for that; but
how about you tell us a little about one of the disciples who is written
about the most in your Gospel and the others—the man Peter?

MATTHEW: It's funny, Mike, but the very first thing that comes to
mind about Peter is that strong accent of his. He had a really strong
north country accent; in fact, I mention this in my Gospel, in chapter
26 verse 73—the bit of the story when he denied knowing Jesus.
Someone had recognized him as a follower of Jesus because of his
strong accent.

As you all know, before Peter became a disciple, he was a hard-
working fisherman. He had a fiery temper—not the sort of man you
would want to upset. He enjoyed his wine. He was happily married.
As you also know, he was a fisherman with his brother Andrew, who
also became a disciple. Andrew had actually been a follower of John
the Baptist, and was delighted to be chosen by Jesus, the man for
whom John had prepared the way.

MIKE: I know that Peter was originally known as Simon, but before
I ask you to explain why Jesus gave him a new name, could you
explain why Jesus also gave you the name Matthew, because you
were always known as Levi, weren't you?

...y case it was quite simple, Mike. Jesus gave me the
...hew, which means 'gift of God'. He gave me this
... of the total change in my character once I started to
...We all know the type of man I was before I met Jesus,
...re we don't want to discuss that again!

Audience laugh.

Going back to Peter, I also need to mention that he had a very warm and caring side to his character. When he was on form, he was wonderful. His faith was so strong. It was this side of Peter that Jesus saw, and because of this, he gave him the new name Peter instead of Simon.[9] Some of us did find this a little amusing at first. I mean, Peter really was a temperamental chap—not the most reliable person—but this was all to change through his close friendship with Jesus.

MIKE: Tell us about that wonderful moment when Jesus renamed Simon; I believe it happened near Caesarea Philippi.

MATTHEW: That's right, Mike. This was another one of those days when we disciples weren't really sure what was going on. Jesus must have known that his time was now running out, and I'm sure he must have been a little concerned that we still didn't truly understand who he was and what it was all about. It wasn't going to be long before he would be leaving his work in our hands!

It was at this place near Caesarea Philippi where Jesus suddenly asked us (and you can read this in my Gospel, chapter 16 verses 13 to 20), 'Who do people say I am?' Well, Mike, some of us told him that folk thought he was John the Baptist, or Elijah, or perhaps Jeremiah or some other prophet. It was then that he asked us directly who we thought he was. Wow! What a question. Who would dare answer such a question? Many of us were beginning to realize and slowly understand who Jesus really was, but it was only Peter who had the faith and guts to answer. He simply replied, 'You're the Messiah, the Son of God.'

MIKE: How did you feel at that moment?

MATTHEW: Throughout our time with Jesus, we had all been slowly struggling to work this out for ourselves—that Jesus truly was the Messiah, the Son of God. It was at this moment that we came a great deal closer to understanding fully what it meant. It was awesome, Mike. We had been chosen by the Son of God to continue his work. At this one point in history, God had chosen this moment to send his Son to proclaim the truth. One moment, I was a pretty unhappy tax collector; the next, I was part of the most fantastic moment in history—face to face with Jesus, the Son of God, finally under-standing who this man really was.

Because of Simon's faith, it was at this moment that Jesus named him Peter. He called him a rock and said that on that rock foundation he would build his Church, and not even death would be able to destroy it. Jesus told Peter that he would give him the keys to the kingdom of heaven. So Peter was made the leader of the Church, which of course you can read about in the book of Acts.

MIKE: Once again, Matthew, thank you so much for sharing with us here this evening. Sadly, we are coming towards the end of the show, but we do have a little more time for perhaps one or two more questions from the audience. Before we do that, I've just received this note from a Roman soldier. Someone's wagon and oxen are blocking the main road in front of the building. If they're not moved in five minutes, the owner will have to pay double the road tax home,[10] and the wagon and animals will be removed.

At this point a little commotion is heard in the middle of the audience, as a fairly young chap, well dressed, dashes to the entrance at the speed of a Roman chariot charging to war. Many of the audience are giggling.

MIKE: Let's hope he can rescue his poor oxen in time. OK, folks, as I said, the show is nearly at an end, but we should have time to sneak in one or two more questions from the audience. Is there anybody who'd like to ask Matthew a final question?

Quite a few hands go up.

MIKE: Right then—the gentleman in the front row, wearing those rather splendid sandals! What's your name, where are you from and what's your question for Matthew?

Hi. My name is Boaz, and I'm from Jerusalem. My question to Matthew is to ask him whether his Gospel is totally his own account of what happened, or did he speak to others or use any other sources to write his Gospel?

MIKE: Now there's a good question, Matthew. Could you give us a brief answer, as we are a little short of time?

MATTHEW: No problem, Mike. Well, as most of you will realize if you've read my Gospel, it actually contains nearly all of Mark's Gospel. The main reason for this is that Mark wrote his Gospel first, and he based it on Peter's teachings.[11] Peter was the leader of us disciples, and he was very close to Jesus. It was vital for me to include in my Gospel anything that Peter said. Because Mark based his entire Gospel on the sayings of Peter, I found this to be such a valuable source for writing my Gospel, which is why most of Mark's Gospel is included in my own.

There was also another collection of Jesus' teachings floating around, and so I used this document to help me write my Gospel.[12] Finally, and I know I am rushed for time, I used some of my own material. There are about 300 verses in my Gospel which you won't find anywhere else. These include many of the Old Testament prophecies that I used, and stories about the birth of Jesus which were my own account of what happened. So in short, my Gospel contains most of the Gospel of Mark, parts of the document containing the teachings of Jesus, and some of my own stuff.

MIKE: A great, straight-to-the-point answer, Matthew. Thank you very much. Sadly, we have come to the end of this first show in the series, *So you think you're a New Testament writer*.

The audience make a lot of noise, shouting, 'Shame!' Others are groaning, showing their disappointment.

What a great first show it's been. Matthew, thank you so much for being our guest. It has been wonderful chatting to you. Also, thank you to the audience. You've been terrific—some great questions!

Matthew, next year there may be another show of some kind which we'd love to invite you to. Thanks for today, and hope to see you next time!

MATTHEW: I've really enjoyed myself, Mike. Thank you so much, and I would love to come on the show again.

A huge round of applause from the audience. They really loved Matthew.

MIKE: Well, that's it, folks. Join us again next week when we welcome our second guest, Mark—also the writer of a Gospel. We really look forward to chatting to him. Thank you all!

---

1 In many cases, one could often tell from what village or area the women came from, by looking at the style of the embroidered edges around their neckline.

2 This passage is from a book in the Apocrypha, which dates from between the Old Testament and the New Testament periods.

3 The best way this can be summed up is through the words of Francis of Assisi.

Lord, make me an instrument of Thy peace;
Where there is hatred, let me sow love;
Where there is injury, pardon;
Where there is discord, union;
Where there is doubt, faith;
Where there is despair, hope;

Where there is darkness, light;
Where there is sadness, joy.

4 Tertullian was to say, 'The blood of the martyrs is the seed of the Church.' Tertullian was an ecclesiastical writer in the second and third centuries. A pagan until middle life, he was converted around AD197 and became a priest.

5 These cast nets were circular nets, often about five metres in diameter, and they had little weights all around the edges. A very long rope was attached to the centre. Whenever a large shoal of fish was seen, the net was dropped over it. Of course, the weights pulled the net down and the fish were trapped underneath. The net was then pulled into shore. In fact, Peter and Andrew were using their cast net when Jesus called them to join him.

6 Cast nets actually dragged everything in from the bottom of the lake, so it was always necessary to separate the good fish from all the rubbish.

7 Mark 3:14–15.

8 The Zealots were a group of fierce Jewish patriots who wished to overthrow the Roman government. They were first-century freedom fighters—or terrorists.

9 The name Peter means 'rock'. It comes from the Greek word *petra*. In Aramaic, which was the language spoken by Jesus, the word was *kephas*.

10 Taxes always had to be paid on a journey. Payment had to be made on all goods, axles, wheels and people travelling, as one passed through different tax districts.

11 We know from a church leader called Papias that Mark was Peter's interpreter.

12 This document has never been found. Today, scholars call it 'Q', which comes from the German word *Quelle*, meaning 'source'. Matthew and Luke both used this source, which helps us understand a little of what was in this original document. Mark did not use 'Q' at all in his Gospel.

Mike Coles chats to Mark

MUSICAL INTRODUCTION

A group of singers walk on to the stage. Two men are holding meziltaim. These are small cymbals made of copper. They were normally banged together in the temple to mark the beginnings, pauses and endings of the verses that were sung.

The group start today's show by singing Psalm 33, a great song of praise.[13] Many of the audience join in. There is a beautiful sound in the courtyard, as everyone makes this joyful noise to God. The banging of the cymbals indicates when they should sing and pause. At the end of the psalm, the group leave the stage and Mike begins the show.

MIKE: Hello again, folks. Welcome to tonight's show, *So you think you're a New Testament writer.* As you might remember, we had a wonderful time last week with Matthew, and this week promises to be just as exciting. Our guest this evening is Mr 'No Nonsense'. His Gospel is the shortest of the four and it is action-packed. It gets straight to the point. So, let's get straight on to tonight's show and welcome our special guest—Mark!

Huge round of applause and plenty of cheering.

MIKE: Mark, can I say what a great pleasure it is to have you on the show tonight, and it's great to see that you are wearing some clothes!

Audience roar with laughter.

MARK: Thanks, Mike! I wondered how long it would take you to bring up that little incident in the garden of Gethsemane, when I ran away naked during the arrest of Jesus.

MIKE: Well, just like you, Mark, I thought I'd get straight to the point! I hope you didn't mind me mentioning it, and if possible I'd like to talk a bit more about that event later in the show.

MARK: Not a problem, Mike, and I would love to chat about that moment in the garden. In fact, that's why I mentioned in my Gospel the bit about me running away naked—to make the point that I was actually there; I saw the whole arrest.

MIKE: We'll certainly chat about it a little later. One thing I'd like to ask you straight away, Mark, is, do you have time to be with us here this evening? The reason I ask is because you use the word 'immediately' 41 times in your Gospel![14] When I read your Gospel, I hardly have a chance to breathe; the whole drama moves at an incredible speed! Why the crazy pace, Mark?

MARK: My 'immediate' response, Mike… no, only joking!

Audience laugh at Mark's sense of humour.

I can't believe it was 41 times I used the word. If my Gospel does have this 'crazy' pace, Mike, it's because I witnessed so much myself —including Jesus' arrest—and that's what it felt like. It was one fantastic miracle after another. Following Jesus when I could was simply awesome. I didn't just write what I saw; my Gospel was mainly based on what Peter told me—his personal memories—and when Peter told me all these things, he spoke nineteen-to-the dozen.

MIKE: Your Gospel certainly is full of action. I suppose you could say that Luke's Gospel is like a history book, Matthew's and John's Gospels are more religious books, but yours is definitely an action-packed thriller! Tell us a little about your main reasons for writing your Gospel, and remember, you have plenty of time—no need to rush.

Audience laugh.

MARK: Just read the first line of my Gospel; that's what it's all about. My Gospel begins, 'This is the good news about Jesus Christ, God's Son.' That's it, folks. My Gospel is a simple piece of writing, mainly based on Peter's memories, telling you all the wonderful news about this man Jesus.

MIKE: Tell us all, Mark, why you don't have any mention of the birth of Jesus in your Gospel, unlike Matthew and Luke.

MARK: I was aware of the miraculous nature of Jesus' birth, but having listened to Peter and after witnessing many of the events myself, I just wanted to get straight to the point about Jesus Christ. I get stuck in straight away with the story of John the Baptist and, to be honest, it's not long before I'm writing about Jesus' final week!

MIKE: It's funny you should say that, because I have heard some folk say that your Gospel is simply a story about the sufferings of Jesus, with a bit of a long introduction!

MARK: Well, that's quite a good way of putting it, I suppose. I do tend to focus on the crucifixion in my Gospel, rather than the actual teaching of Jesus. I also tend to focus on Jesus' actions rather than his teachings. Listening to Peter's accounts, I was always being told about what Jesus did, and of course the greatest thing that Jesus *did* for us was to die on the cross for us all, to defeat death and give us the chance to receive eternal life. This was the most amazing action in history!

Many of the audience shout 'Amen' here, and the applause is deafening.

I'm told that at least one-third of my Gospel deals with the miracles of Jesus. These miracles were most certainly central to the life of Jesus. So again, it's the actions of Jesus that concern me.

MIKE: Thanks very much for that, Mark. In a moment, folks, I'll let some of you ask Mark some questions if you have any. There were certainly plenty of questions for Matthew last week. But before that, a little advert.

Two men walk across the stage carrying a large canvas of the type used for making tents. On it have been painted the words:

THE BEST OLIVE OIL IN TOWN!

One of the men then says, 'Hi. My name's Barnabas. I grow and press the finest olives around. If it's olives you want to eat with your barley bread at breakfast,[15] or olive oil for cooking, or for fuel for your lamps, or soap, or if you want to give your skin and hair a real shine, then come and see me after the show with a few shekels and I'm sure I can do you a good deal! Before I leave, here you go, Mike and Mark—a bottle each of my finest oil. Enjoy!'

Mike and Mark are very grateful. The audience applaud Barnabas as he leaves.

MARK: What a lovely chap, and how kind. This oil looks great. Should keep my hair looking shiny for the next few months!

MIKE: I use a fair bit of oil on my hair as well, Mark. Healthy stuff, you know. But this is beginning to turn into a fashion show, so let's get straight back to the questions. As I said before the advert, we'll now go over to the audience. Would anyone like to ask Mark a question?

Quite a few hands go up.

MIKE: The lady on the second row from the back, in the green—yes, you, madam.

'My name is Saul! I'm a man!'

MIKE: I do apologize, Saul. My sight isn't what it used to be!

Audience laugh.

What is your question for Mark, Saul?

'Hello, Mark. It's good to be here today listening to you. In your Gospel, you brilliantly make the point that Jesus was an ordinary human being, and yet you also show us that he was the Son of God. Was it your aim to get these two points across?'

MARK: Thank you for your kind words and your question, Saul. It was most certainly my aim to make these two points. Jesus was truly a human being, and you see that many times in my Gospel. For example, in chapter 4 verses 35 to 41, you can read about the miracle when Jesus calmed a storm. But before he did the miracle, Jesus was in a really deep sleep in the boat because he was so exhausted. Yes, Jesus got tired like the rest of us.

Also like the rest of us, Jesus got fed up and annoyed. A classic example of this is recorded in my Gospel, chapter 8 verses 14 to 21. Here you can read how, once again, the disciples had failed to understand what Jesus was teaching. He actually said to them, 'Do you lot still not understand anything? Are your minds so blank?' Pretty strong words, but again the point I'm making here is that Jesus was fully human. One more powerful example showing the humanness of Jesus is when he was in the garden of Gethsemane. Here I record how he was full of fear about what was going to happen to him. He really was suffering. In chapter 14, I record that during this time in the garden, Jesus was desperate for the company of some of his disciples, but each time he went to them, they were asleep.

This saddened Jesus even more. It makes me shiver just talking about this incident. I was there that evening. Jesus was so lonely, so frightened. His disciples and us followers, we all let him down in what was such a dark moment for him.

So Jesus truly was fully human, but as Saul mentioned, my aim is also to show that Jesus is the Son of God. I demonstrate this point clearly in the beginning, middle and end of my Gospel—quite clever, I thought!

Audience chuckle a little as Mark gives himself a bit of praise.

The obvious and main point of my Gospel is to tell the world that Jesus was the Son of God, so what better way than to repeat it at the beginning, middle and end of the Gospel?

In the beginning, at Jesus' baptism it is revealed that Jesus is God's Son. After he had been baptized, and was coming out of the water, a voice from heaven said, 'You are my own dear Son. I am so pleased with you.' How much clearer could it be than that?

MIKE: Not much!

MARK: Then, halfway through the Gospel, in chapter 9 verses 2 to 8, there was Jesus' transfiguration, when he was up a mountain with some of his disciples, and a voice clearly said from a cloud, 'This is my Son. Listen to him.'

The final event that I record in my Gospel to make this point is at Jesus' crucifixion, in chapter 15 verse 39. It was the amazing moment when the army officer who had been standing in front of the cross when Jesus died looked up and said, 'This man truly was the Son of God.' That was a very powerful moment when even an ordinary Roman soldier recognized who Jesus really was.

MIKE: Saul, thanks very much for that great question. Mark, it's wonderful how you reveal to us in your Gospel these two characteristics of who Jesus was—a real human being and the Son of

God. OK, I'd like us to move straight on to another question. The lady (and this time I'm certain it's a lady) in the third row, wearing purple. What's your name and what is your question for Mark?

'My name is Martha. I'm from Sepphoris. I know we all laughed at the beginning of the show about the fact that it's good to see Mark wearing clothes today, but it must have been an awful time in the garden that night when Jesus was arrested. Could you tell us about that experience and describe how you felt?'

MIKE: An excellent question, Martha. I said we'd get round to talking about this incident during the show, so now would be a good time. Mark, would you be happy to share your account of that terrible night?

MARK: Of course I would, Mike, and thank you, Martha, for asking me the question.

I'd just like to set the scene for you. As I've said, most of my Gospel is based on Peter's account of what happened. Peter explained to me that before they reached the garden of Gethsemane, the disciples had just eaten the Passover meal with Jesus, when the whole meal was given a totally new meaning. Jesus was now to be seen as the Passover lamb, and the bread would represent his body, which was to be sacrificed, and the wine his blood, which was to be poured out for many people. After the meal, Peter explained that they sang a hymn and then set out for the Mount of Olives. It was as they were on their way there that I joined the group, along with others who tended to follow Jesus around.

As we were walking, Jesus was telling his disciples how they were all going to abandon him. He quoted from the scripture which said that the shepherd would be killed and all the sheep would run away, obviously meaning that Jesus was to be killed and his disciples would flee. I remember Peter shouting at Jesus, telling him how he would never leave Jesus, not in a million years. He said that all the other disciples might run off, but he would never do such a thing. I heard

Jesus reply that before the cock crowed twice that evening, Peter would have denied ever knowing Jesus, and that he would do this three times.

When the group reached Gethsemane, Jesus took Peter, James and John with him and they went off to pray in a quiet place. Peter told me that Jesus had said how awful and sad he felt. He said that the sorrow was crushing him, and asked the three of them to keep watch as he prayed. Peter could hear Jesus pleading with his Father[16] that he might be spared 'this cup of suffering', but only if it could be done in accordance with God's will.

At this point, Mark pauses. He is clearly struggling with his emotions as he remembers this terrible experience. The audience are silent. Eventually, he is able to continue.

Peter told me that not long after hearing Jesus praying, he and the other two fell asleep. When Jesus returned, Jesus was quite disappointed, asking his friends why they couldn't even stay awake for one hour. He reminded them of the importance of prayer, as 'the spirit is willing but the flesh is weak'.

I remember Peter being very upset when he told me about this incident. He felt that he had really let Jesus down. Jesus was obviously in a terrible state, so sad and lonely. Peter kept telling me how he should have been there for Jesus, comforting and supporting him, but instead he fell asleep. It didn't happen just once either, but three times!

While all this was going on, I was actually asleep myself, and as it was such a warm evening, I had slipped out of my robe and was simply lying underneath it. The next thing I remember is waking up to complete chaos. I looked up and saw Judas with Jesus. There was a large crowd there all armed with clubs and swords. They had come to arrest Jesus and anyone else who was with him. I saw someone cut off the high priest's slave's ear with a sword. That's when the disciples panicked and ran away. I was terrified and I just stood up and ran. I didn't have my robe on, as I explained, and the little bit of linen cloth I also had wrapped around me just fell away. I was so confused and scared, I didn't care. I just ran.

At this point it is clear to see that Mark has a tear in his eye. He stops talking, obviously quite upset.

MIKE: It's sounds like a terrible time, Mark. Thank you so much for sharing it with us here today. I can bet that every one of us here would have done exactly the same thing—just run away in pure confusion and terror. Jesus knew this; he said that all the disciples would scatter, including Peter, despite his denial that he could ever do such a thing.

The audience give a huge round of applause, showing their love and total support for Mark.

MARK: Thank you so much, all of you. The silly thing is that Jesus said many times that he would be arrested and led off to die, but the disciples and many of his followers never really understood him. So when it actually happened, we were shocked and terrified. To be honest, we thought he would use his powers as the Messiah to save himself. But that wasn't his way. It was only afterwards, after his resurrection, that we really understood Jesus' mission here on earth.

There is suddenly a huge commotion at the back. Ten Roman soldiers storm into the building.

MIKE: Oh no! Now what?

One of the soldiers shouts out, 'We're so sorry to interrupt your little religious show, but we have heard that there may be one or two Zealots hiding here among your audience. I'm sure you won't mind if we have a look.'

MIKE: I don't really have much choice, do I? All I want is a peaceful show. Is that too much to ask? Have a look around, but I can tell you now, we have no people of violence here today. We love our enemies! God bless you all!

The soldiers stomp around for a while, looking at each row of people very closely. After a while, they obviously haven't found who they're looking for, and with no apology at all they just storm out of the building as loudly as they stormed in.

MIKE: Charming!

Audience laugh.

MIKE: Well, I'm very sorry about that, Mark, but you know what the Romans can be like!

MARK: Yes, we know what they're like, but we love them all and pray for them.

MIKE: We mentioned earlier in the show that much of your Gospel is about what Jesus did rather than what he said, and that at least a third of your Gospel deals with the miracles that Jesus performed. While Peter was telling you his account of his time with Jesus, did he ever mention which of the miracles he found most incredible?

MARK: The way Peter spoke to me, it was clear that every second he spent with Jesus was amazing. He spoke with real emotion about every miracle he described, but I do remember him being especially excited when he told me about Jairus' daughter being raised from the dead.

MIKE: Could you tell us about that miracle today?

MARK: I'd be happy to, Mike.

Peter told me how Jesus and the disciples were by the side of Lake Galilee, and as usual there was a large crowd. An official of the local synagogue turned up. His name was Jairus. Peter explained that the first thing Jairus did when he saw Jesus was to fall at his feet and start telling Jesus that his daughter was really ill. He begged Jesus to lay his hands on his daughter and heal her. It wasn't long after this that some messengers came from Jairus' house to bring the sad news that the little girl had died, and that he needn't bother Jesus any more.

I remember Peter telling me that he was quite amazed at Jesus' response to this: all Jesus said was, 'Don't worry, just believe.'

Jesus then took Peter, James and John into the house. Peter said that the atmosphere was awful. There were people crying and wailing—total confusion. Again, Jesus surprised everyone by saying, 'What's all this crying and confusion for? The child isn't dead, she's just sleeping!'

Peter told me that this didn't really help matters at that particular moment. You don't go to someone's house where a young child has just died and tell everyone she's only sleeping. It's not really the done thing!

Audience laugh.

But what happened next was truly remarkable, Peter told me. Jesus went up to where the girl was lying, took her by the hand and said, '*Talitha koum.*'[17] Peter was in the room with Jesus, and he said there was no doubt that the girl was dead. As soon as Jesus had spoken these words, though, she just got up and started walking around. I remember that as Peter was telling me this, he was shaking his head in amazement, as if he was there again. He had witnessed the most awesome power of God—power even over death itself. As you can imagine, everyone was astonished when they saw the girl walk out of the room. They just stood there and stared in silence for a few moments. Jesus told them to feed the girl, and he made his usual request for people not to tell anyone what they had seen.

MIKE: That brings me on to an interesting point, Mark. Why did Jesus always ask people not to tell anyone what they had seen him do? I can imagine *that* being impossible! If I had seen any of the miracles he performed, I can assure you, I'd have to tell everyone! It almost seems like some sort of messianic secret—him not wanting people to know who he really is.

MARK: I like your phrase, 'messianic secret'! That's basically what it was all about. As you all know, people expected the Messiah to be a politically powerful figure, setting up his kingdom here on earth and destroying his enemies. But Jesus did not want people to see him as this sort of Messiah, so early on in his ministry. People may have tried to make him king, and if that had happened his whole mission might have ended in disaster. It was for this simple reason that he had to try to keep his actions secret for as long as possible.

At this point, somebody from the audience suddenly runs down to where Mike and Mark are sitting. He is carrying a goatskin bottle of wine.

'I'm so sorry to disturb the show like this. My name is Jeremiah. I own a winepress and make my own wine. It's such an honour to be here today, and I just wanted to share some good wine with you.'

MIKE: Most excellent, Jeremiah. I don't mind these sorts of interruptions, and I'm sure Mark doesn't either.

MARK: Absolutely not.

Jeremiah produces two cups and pours some wine into each one. Mike and Mark simultaneously say 'To life',[18] and take a sip.

MARK: Wonderful stuff, Jeremiah! Thank you so much. My, my, this reminds me of the psalmist thanking God for the gift of wine that makes him happy.[19]

MIKE: Or when Isaac blesses Jacob and says, 'May the Lord give you plenty of corn and wine!'[20]

They toast each other again and finish the cups. They thank Jeremiah; the audience give him a big round of applause, and he sits back down, leaving the wineskin with Mike and Mark.

Hey, Jeremiah's left the wineskin behind. What I think we might do is that, at the end of the show, I'll set a little question—something to do with Mark's Gospel—and whoever gets it right wins the wine. What do you think of that, folks?

A big cheer from the audience. A few shout out, 'Praise the Lord!'

MIKE: Getting back to more serious issues for a moment, Mark, a few people asked me before the show to focus in on chapter 10 verse 45 of your Gospel, where you write, 'The Son of Man did not come to be served; but he came to serve and to give his life to redeem many people.' In light of this very powerful verse, what would you say was the main reason for the work and purpose of Jesus?

MARK: After listening to Peter's account, and having been part of the large crowd that often followed Jesus, I have to say that Jesus' ministry should be seen in terms of the 'suffering servant' described in Isaiah 53. By the way, this links in with what we were discussing earlier about the messianic secret. Jesus was not going to be a powerful political Messiah, but a suffering Messiah as portrayed in Isaiah's prophecy. This is why Jesus had to keep things secret for as long as possible, as I'm sure most people would never have understood the idea of God's Messiah having to suffer and die. But, if people truly had understood the passage in Isaiah, they would have realized that this was God's plan from the beginning.

Would you mind, Mike, if I were to recite parts of Isaiah 53 to make this point?

MIKE: We would all love to hear some of that wonderful passage.

MARK: It says, 'He endured the suffering that should have been ours. He suffered the pain that we should have suffered. Because of our sins he was beaten and wounded. We are all healed by the punishment he suffered. Like a lamb led out to be slaughtered, he never said a word. He was arrested, sentenced and led out to die, and no one cared. He was put to death for the sins of the people. The Lord says, "It was my will that he should suffer; his death was a sacrifice to bring forgiveness for all."'[21]

MIKE: Fantastic stuff. Jesus' death really was a cosmic event.

MARK: Indeed it was, Mike. The result of our wrongdoing would always be death—Satan's greatest weapon. But Jesus destroyed death! For, as we all know, three days after his death on the cross, Jesus rose again. He defeated death, and thanks to that, we can now conquer death if we believe and trust in Jesus as our Saviour. We're the ones who should go through all that pain and suffering. We're the ones who should be led off like sheep to be slaughtered. We're the sinners! But no, God loved us so much that he let his Son endure the pain and suffering, even though he was perfect.

The audience really applaud here, and many shout out 'Alleluia!'

You know, when I was in the garden of Gethsemane that night when Jesus was arrested, it all seemed so confusing. None of us really understood the true nature of Jesus' mission. It was so awful to see him arrested and led off like a sheep to be slaughtered.

But of course, it makes sense now. Despite what happened, despite me running away naked in terror, we all know that Jesus rose from the dead in glory. Jesus our king has conquered the greatest enemy of all—death. Amen to that!

'Amen to that!' shout all the audience.

MIKE: Absolutely! Amen to that! If you don't mind, Mark, I'd like to go back to the arrest in the garden. The authorities obviously knew Jesus was there because Judas had led them there. What did Peter tell you about Judas?

MARK: I can tell you now that at the time of the arrest, Peter hated Judas! Even before then, Peter had never trusted Judas—he described him to me as a very dodgy character. Peter even told me that when they were eating the Passover meal together, Jesus had said that he would be betrayed by one of the disciples, and that it would be better for that person to have never been born! He also told me that Judas was a bit of a thief, nicking cash from the disciples' moneybag.

When Peter looked back at the whole sequence of events, though, there was no hatred there any more, just pity. I suppose we also have to remember that it was God's plan for Jesus to be arrested and led off to die, as prophesied in Isaiah 53.

MIKE: I was given a couple of questions about Judas before the show, from various members of the audience: 'What did Judas do that was so bad?' and 'Why exactly do you think Judas betrayed Jesus?'

MARK: As far as the first question is concerned, you have to remember that the religious leaders of Israel who absolutely hated Jesus had a bit of a problem. They wanted Jesus arrested and put to death as soon as possible, but they couldn't just walk up to him in the middle of the street and do it, because Jesus was so popular. Because it was the time of the Passover festival, there were thousands of pilgrims camped out all over the place, and so they couldn't arrest Jesus secretly either, because they had no idea where he and his disciples were staying. It's here, of course, that Judas comes into the story. In my Gospel, I write in chapter 14 verses 10 and 11, how Judas went off to the chief priests in order to betray Jesus to them. They offered him thirty pieces of silver. It was that same night that Judas led the authorities to Jesus in the garden—the betrayal.

The second question is a lot trickier for me to answer. There are a few possibilities as to why Judas betrayed Jesus.

The first and most obvious reason is that Judas did it for the money! As I mentioned earlier, he was known to have stolen money from the disciples. But I often wonder whether he really did it just for that. I mean, thirty pieces of silver wasn't actually a great deal of money. Could anyone betray a friend to certain death for just thirty pieces of silver? I don't really think this was his motive.

When I was chatting to Peter about this, we often wondered whether Judas did it simply because he was scared. The disciples all knew that the authorities were out to get Jesus, and maybe Judas thought he would end up in trouble as one of Jesus' disciples, so he thought he'd betray him and save his own skin.

But I honestly believe that Judas betrayed Jesus because he was disappointed with him. Jesus was the Son of God, the Messiah, but he wasn't behaving like a Messiah should. Judas wanted Jesus to be a political Messiah, and I guess he thought that if he put Jesus in a really tight spot, then perhaps he might reveal his messianic power. But of course, this didn't happen. That's why Judas felt so awful afterwards; full of remorse, he killed himself. I suppose, in a way, I feel sorry for Judas. There were many times when we wanted Jesus to fit the description of the political Messiah that Israel was always hoping for. Poor Judas just took things too far—a sad, misguided chap.

MIKE: Thanks for that, Mark. I'd just assumed, as perhaps many do, that Judas did it for the money. You've certainly made things much clearer.

Do you fancy another glass of that most excellent wine?

MARK: You bet! But we mustn't have too much; remember, you were going to give it away as a prize at the end of the show.

MIKE: Oh, did I really say that?

'Oh yes, you did!' shout several members of the audience.

Yes, it's coming back to me. I did promise that, didn't I? Well, just a little glass each then.

Sadly, Mark, we are coming to the end of this week's show, but we do have a bit of time left. I think we'll go back to the audience and get a question or two from them. Would anyone like to ask Mark a question?

How about the lady in the front wearing the lovely blue tunic?

'Hi. My name's Elizabeth, and I'm from Jerusalem. As we know, the Romans are treating us followers of Christ pretty terribly. Do you have any words of comfort for us, Mark?'

MARK: As many of you are aware, Nero blamed Christians for the fire in Rome. When we meet to share the Lord's supper, the Romans think that we're a bunch of cannibals meeting together to eat 'flesh' and drink 'blood'. Also, Christians are refusing to burn incense to honour the emperor as a god. This, Elizabeth, is why we're being treated so badly. The words of comfort I have for you folks are in my Gospel. By writing it, I'm hoping to encourage you all to hold on to your faith in these bad times. Something that you can read in my Gospel, which may comfort and strengthen you, Elizabeth, is the story I mentioned before, of that wonderful miracle when Jesus calmed a storm. It's in the fourth chapter, verses 35 to 41.

Jesus had told his disciples to get into the boat and cross over Lake Galilee. It wasn't long before they hit some awful weather. Huge waves were smashing into the boat, and plenty of water was spilling over the sides. While all this was happening, Jesus was sleeping in the back of the boat with his head on a pillow. The disciples were in a terrible state; they woke Jesus and cried out to him, 'Teacher, don't you care that we're going to die?' Jesus just stood up and said to the wind, 'Be quiet!' and to the waves, 'Be still!' Within a few seconds the wind had died down, and it became completely calm. Jesus then said to the disciples, 'Why are you so frightened? Do you lot still not have any faith?'

They were terrified. They couldn't understand who this man really was—a man with power over the wind and waves.

The point of this story, Elizabeth, is that for you and many Christians at the moment it may seem as if God is asleep. We are all going through 'storms', and many of us may wonder where God is. In the story, Jesus didn't save the disciples from the storm, but he was with them in the storm.

It's the same with us, Elizabeth. We mustn't be frightened or lose our faith as the disciples did. Christ is with us too, to comfort and protect us.

'Thank you so much, Mark. You can't imagine how helpful your words are for me. God bless you!'

MIKE: I would like to echo what Elizabeth just said. Those were powerful words of comfort, Mark. Thank you for sharing them with us.

The audience really applaud.

There's one question I'd like to ask Mark quickly as we're almost at the end of the show, and we still have to set a question to see who wins the wine. Maybe it's because I'm a little dopey, but throughout your Gospel, Jesus is referred to as the Son of Man, the Son of David, Christ, Messiah and Saviour. Could you just briefly explain what these different titles actually mean?

MARK: I think it's important to understand the significance of each of these titles used for Jesus. I'll keep it short, and Mike, of course you're not dopey. I think it's a great question.

If I could start with the 'Son of Man'. This is the title that Jesus uses when he refers to himself. It obviously gets across the point that Jesus felt ordinary human emotions. It is also used by Jesus to claim that he is the great leader mentioned by the prophet Daniel. In the book of Daniel,[22] which was written to encourage the people at a time of persecution, the writer describes a number of visions which show that God will eventually save and restore his people. In one vision, he describes the 'Son of Man' coming with the clouds of heaven, and he says that this Son of Man would have great authority from God.

Another title of Jesus is 'Son of David'. In my Gospel, chapter 10 verses 46 to 52, I record the miracle when Jesus healed the blind man Bartimaeus. Bartimaeus was sitting by the side of the road when he heard that Jesus was approaching. He shouted out a few times, 'Jesus! Son of David! Take pity on me!' and Jesus healed him because of his faith. The great thing about Bartimaeus is that even though he was blind, the fact that he referred to Jesus as the Son of David shows that he could still 'see' who Jesus really was.

To discover the real significance of this title, the 'Son of David', we need to go back a thousand years. God had spoken to King David, the greatest king the Jews had ever had, through the prophet Nathan. God had said that David's family line would never die out and his kingdom and his throne would last for all time.[23] Because of this, many Jews expected that when the Messiah came, he would be exactly like King David—a royal leader who would defeat Israel's enemies, so that Israel would once more become a great nation.

The words 'Christ' and 'Messiah' both mean 'anointed one'. In Old Testament times, all kings and priests were anointed with oil when they took office: they were the 'anointed ones'. Throughout Israel's troubled history, the Jews expected that God would send his own 'anointed one', the Messiah. It's actually a woman at Bethany who anoints Jesus by pouring perfume over his body. As we have mentioned before, Mike, although Jesus saw himself as the Messiah, he was not the type of Messiah that most Jews were expecting. He was not going to be a warrior king, or a great prophet like Moses.

I'm conscious of the time, Mike, and I hope that my brief answer helps to explain the meaning of some of these titles of Jesus.

MIKE: Once again, Mark, a wonderful answer; and yes, we are sadly coming to the end of the show.

Audience start to boo; they don't want the show to end.

I know, I'm sorry, folks. I could sit and chat to Mark for ever. But before we round things up, I'm going to ask Mark whether he could set us a little question based on his Gospel—and, of course, the winner gets the wine courtesy of Jeremiah.

The audience all turn to Jeremiah and give him a huge cheer and round of applause.

So Mark, what's the question? The first person to put their hand up and give the correct answer wins this wonderful wine.

MARK: OK, Mike, here it is: When a teacher of the Law asked Jesus what the most important commandment was, Jesus replied, 'Hear, O Israel! The Lord our God is the only Lord. Love the Lord your God with all your heart, with all your soul, with all your mind and with all your strength.'[24] My question to you is, 'What did Jesus say was the second most important commandment?'

Immediately a young woman in the front row puts her hand up to answer.

MIKE: Well, without a shadow of a doubt, although many hands have gone up, the quickest was the young lady sat here in the front row. What's your name, and more importantly, what do you think the answer to Mark's question is?

'Hi. My name is Rachel. Jesus' second commandment was that we should love our neighbours as much as we love ourselves!'

MARK: Absolutely correct!

The audience give Rachel a huge round of applause.

MIKE: Well done, Rachel. Come and collect your wine, you lucky thing. What a way to end the show, to hear the words that we should love our neighbours as we love ourselves.

Can I say, Mark, what a great pleasure it has been having you on the show this week. I'm sure the audience would love to show their appreciation.

The audience give Mark prolonged applause, and there is plenty of loud cheering.

MARK: Thank you for having me on the show, and thank you all for making me so welcome. I've really enjoyed it.

MIKE: Perhaps we'll see you again some time in the future. Mark, thank you.

That's the end of another great show. Next week I'm delighted to say that we have Luke on the show as our special guest. Yes, folks, we'll have a doctor in the house! Thanks for joining us tonight. Hope to see you all next week on *So you think you're a New Testament writer*.

---

13 James said that the singing of psalms expresses our happiness (James 5:13).

14 The Greek word for this is *euthus*.

15 A typical working man's breakfast.

16 Jesus uses the word 'Abba' for Father, demonstrating his childlike attitude of trust in his Father.

17 This means, 'Little girl, I tell you to get up!'

18 This is the Jewish equivalent of people in Britain saying 'Cheers!'

19 Psalm 104:15.

20 Genesis 27:28.

21 Parts of Isaiah 53:4–10.

22 Daniel 7:13–14.

23 2 Samuel 7:16.

24 Mark 12:29–30.

Mike Coles chats to Luke

MUSICAL INTRODUCTION

A man and a woman walk on to the stage. The man is holding a halil. This was a pipe bored out of either wood or bone. The name actually comes from the verb halil, *which means 'to bore'. This instrument needed a reed to produce the sound, which was normally carried around in a pouch. It made quite a light sound. The halil was never played in worship, but was simply used by ordinary people.*

In today's musical introduction, the pipe is played and the woman dances to the tune. Dance was always just as important as music during biblical times. Miriam led a celebration of singing and dancing when the Hebrews had safely crossed the Red Sea (Exodus 15:21). In 2 Samuel 6:14–15, we can read how David danced in front of the ark of the covenant as it was brought back to Jerusalem.

At the end of the dance, the audience applaud enthusiastically. Then Mike starts the show.

MIKE: Well, ladies and gentlemen, can you believe it? Here we are again; it's the third in our series, *So you think you're a New Testament writer*. We've had two wonderful shows so far, chatting to Matthew and then Mark. Tonight's show promises to be just as exciting. Please put your hands together and welcome that wonderful doctor, and writer of a Gospel and the book of Acts—Luke!

The audience go wild. There are far more women in the crowd than usual, and quite a few 'down and outs', and all of them give Luke an incredible welcome, which goes on for quite a while. Mike is unable to say anything until the noise eventually dies down.

MIKE: Wow! What a reception, Luke.

LUKE: Wonderful! It's a great pleasure to be here. God bless you all.

The audience applaud once again.

MIKE: I don't think I've ever known anyone receive a welcome like that. Looking around tonight's absolutely packed-out audience, I can see loads of women, quite a few tax collectors, and over there at the back, in their own little section, are some lepers. Would it be fair to say, Luke, that it was all these folk that Jesus came to love and care for, according to your Gospel?

LUKE: That's exactly the message of my Gospel, Mike.

MIKE: I would like to focus on that in a moment, but before we do, you couldn't quickly look in my mouth, could you, Doc? I've had an awful toothache for days, and wondered whether you could help.

Luke has a quick look in Mike's mouth.

LUKE: I think I can see the problem, Mike. One of those back teeth of yours looks pretty rotten. What I might do after the show is to get you to drink some wine mixed with myrrh. That will help reduce the pain, and then I'll pull that tooth out for you.

MIKE: Well, I can't say I'm looking forward to that, but thank you very much, Luke. Now we all know that you were Paul's doctor and friend. In fact, he referred to you as 'dear Dr Luke'.[25] Could you tell us a little about what it's like to be a doctor, and your views on medicine?

LUKE: First of all, Mike, don't worry about your tooth. We'll have that sorted out in no time.

As for me being a doctor, I think it's important for people to realize that I am a Gentile. As you all know, in the Old Testament view of sickness and disease, people believed that there was a connection between disease and sin and spirit possession, and because of that belief, medicine and medical practice did not really develop among the Jews. But I am a Greek, and trained to be a doctor in Greece, where medicine has made great advances. I had to follow the teachings of Hippocrates, and took an oath that the life of a patient should come first. I also swore that I would never take advantage of women, never perform an abortion and always keep patients' medical details confidential.

MIKE: It just dawned on me, Luke, that perhaps it's because of your background as a doctor, and the oath you had to swear, that you are such a wonderful, caring person, and that might explain why you got such a great welcome from the audience!

Luke, you mentioned the Old Testament view of disease being linked to sin and spirit possession, which meant that medicine wasn't really trusted, but what about Jesus? What was his attitude?

LUKE: Well, Jesus also accepted to some extent that diseases could be caused by spirit possession, and dealt with them in that way when he had to, but Jesus did not 'cast out demons' every time he came across someone with a disease. Thanks to his attitude towards sickness and disease, we doctors began to be accepted in the Church, and, as you mentioned earlier, Paul called me 'his dear doctor'.

MIKE: I thought I'd ask you first about being a doctor, because I think it links in with your concern to show in your Gospel how Jesus loved and cared for the outcasts in society. The people here have shown how much they really love you, so before we talk about your reasons for writing your Gospel, could we focus on this sympathy you seem to have for the underdog?

LUKE: Of course we could, my dear Mike. The simple point I make in my Gospel is how Jesus cared for the weak and poor in society. It is they who are close to receiving the good news, rather than the rich. Remember how, in my Gospel, Mary, when she is pregnant with Jesus, sings, 'He has filled the hungry with good things, and he's sent the rich away with nothing.'[26] Also, when Jesus first starts his work, I record how he says, 'The Spirit of the Lord is upon me, because he has chosen me to bring good news to all the poor.'[27] So in these two passages alone we can see that it was Jesus' mission to show the love of God to the poor and outcasts in society.

MIKE: I earn a fair bit of money, Luke. Does that mean I'll never know God's love, or that the good news is not for me?

LUKE: I think you're quite a humble chap, Mike, judging by the way you dress and the manner in which you speak, and that's what it's all about. There should be no love of money or riches. I know a few people who are quite well off but who have good hearts, and spend much of their time helping others. They know that God has blessed them with a lot of money. They know that it all comes from him, and that's what counts. Nothing ultimately belongs to us, and if we have been blessed with much, it is our duty to help those with little.

MIKE: Could you remind us of that wonderful parable Jesus told about the rich fool?

LUKE: Of course, Mike. That's a perfect example of the dangers of being greedy and just thinking about yourself. Jesus told a story about a rich man whose land always bore excellent crops. He started to wonder where he could store his harvest, and decided to tear down his barns and build even bigger ones for all his corn and other goods. He thought that if he did this, he would have all the good things he would ever need for many years. He could eat, drink and enjoy himself. But God thought that the man was a fool! He said to him, 'Tonight you are going to lose your life. Who will now get all the wealth that you have been keeping to yourself?' Jesus ended by saying that this is what will happen to those who just pile up riches for themselves, but who in God's eyes have empty hearts.

The audience applaud here, obviously pleased to hear this parable and the important message behind it.

MIKE: So that's the rich and poor, but what about the outcast folk? Do we have any tax collectors or Samaritans in here?

Quite a few members of the audience wave a hand.

There you go, Luke, there are quite a few so-called 'outcasts' with us this evening, and I know that, sat at the very back in their own little corner, we have some lepers who've come to listen to you today.

'Oi, Mike! Less of the "outcasts", if you don't mind! We've been called outcasts all our lives; we didn't come to your show today to be called outcasts again!' shouts one of the audience.

MIKE: In no way did I mean to upset anyone here today. When I use the term 'outcast', it's only to make the point that this is how society *used* to see you, but Jesus changed all that. This is what we want to affirm here, and praise the Lord for that!

'Amen!' shout many of the audience.

Luke, tell us more about Jesus mixing with these so-called 'outcasts'.

LUKE: We know that Jesus mixed with all sorts in society—taxmen, criminals and prostitutes! Society may have had a problem with this, but Jesus certainly didn't. These were the people who really needed his help, and I have every understanding and sympathy with this, having been a slave myself.[28] It makes me sick to think that so-called religious people could despise these groups in society who, more than anything, needed to be loved and cared for, not hated, despised and spat on!

Huge cheer from the audience when Luke says this.

As I've recorded Jesus saying in my Gospel, chapter 19 verse 10, 'The Son of Man has come to seek and save the lost.'

MIKE: Could you give us some examples, Luke, from your Gospel, where Jesus does seem to stick up for the 'underdog' in society?

LUKE: I'd be delighted to, Mike. I'll use three examples, if that's all right with you—taxmen, Samaritans,[29] and lepers.

We'll start with taxmen. I don't need to say much about them as you dealt with this topic in some detail when you interviewed Matthew, but we all know that most taxmen had an awful reputation for being greedy and dishonest. In my Gospel, chapter 18 verses 9 to 14, I tell the wonderful parable of the Pharisee and the tax collector who both go off to the temple to pray. The Pharisee stands there on his own, really full of himself, thanking God that he isn't greedy, dishonest or an adulterer. He thanks God that he is not like the tax collector who is also praying in the temple. He boasts about how he fasts two days a week and gives away a tenth of all his income.

The tax collector, on the other hand, just stands there beating his breast, not even able to look up to heaven. He asks God to have pity on him, as he is a sinner. After telling this parable, Jesus makes it quite clear that it is the tax collector who is right with God, not the Pharisee. All those who are full of themselves and make themselves look great are going to be humbled, and those who humble themselves will be made great.

Suddenly, five men get up from the audience and run down to where Mike and Luke are sitting on the stage. They kneel in front of Luke and one of them says, 'Luke, we're tax collectors. We're greedy, and we cheat folk all the time. This is not how we want to be. Please help us. We know we've done wrong; we want to change. What must we do?'

MIKE: Well, there's never a dull moment on this show!

LUKE: Could I just say how wonderful it is that you five men have been brave enough to come forward like this. You ask me what you must do; well, you've pretty much done it. You've come to realize that the way you were carrying on was dishonest and you want to change. That's all Jesus would ever ask someone to do. That's what Matthew did. If you are truly sorry for your greedy past, if you accept that Jesus is God's Son and that he came to help and love people like you, then you are saved, my brothers. Go out and share your stolen riches with those who really need it. Join our Christian family.

The five men are in tears. They seem touched by the love of God, so that their hearts have changed. The audience stand and applaud, and some people run down to the five men and hug them and welcome them into the Christian family. Then they escort the men back to their seats, praising God as they do.

MIKE: Amazing stuff! The power of the gospel at work in tonight's show! Luke, could you now tell us a little about Jesus' revolutionary attitude to the Samaritans?

LUKE: I'll just remind people, Mike, that the Jews have always regarded the Samaritans as enemies. It all started about 700 years ago, when the Assyrians had conquered the northern part of Palestine. What the Assyrians used to do, to prevent rebellion in the lands they had conquered, was to move part of the population elsewhere and then import other peoples into the newly conquered area. The Samaritans are descendants of Jews who had intermarried with foreigners during this time and they now form a separate community living in the middle of Palestine. The Jews really do hate them, and quite often will make detours on a journey to avoid passing through Samaritan areas. What did Jesus say about this enmity between them? Well, he was disgusted. One of his best-known parables, only told in my Gospel, in chapter 10 verses 30 to 37, is the story of the good Samaritan. This is quite clearly an anti-racist parable, with a Samaritan as the hero. This came as a huge shock to Jesus' listeners. He was simply making the point that we are all equal, no matter who we are, where we're from, or what colour we are.

Again, the audience really love this, and give Luke a massive round of applause.

MIKE: Thanks, Luke. I've just had it signalled to me that it's time for our little advert. Back in a few moments. Don't go away!

Four men appear on the stage. They all shout out in unison:

'DO YOU NEED A DECENT PACK ANIMAL? THEN GET YOUR DONKEYS FROM ME! YOU WON'T FIND BETTER!'

As soon as they've finished shouting, another chap appears and says, 'Hi everyone. My name's Abraham. I've been breeding donkeys for many years now. I know that most of us here rely on these wonderful animals to transport us around, as well as our bits and pieces. Some of us may harness our donkeys to corn mills or water wheels, and one or two of us just love to own one of these little animals as pets, especially for the kids. Let me show you some of my finest specimens at the moment.'

Four donkeys are brought into the building by some of Abraham's friends. The donkeys walk in calmly and peacefully. They are fine animals with beautiful bright eyes and alert expressions.

'As you can see, ladies and gentlemen, they are lovely animals, and I know you won't find better in this area. After the show, I will be outside with a wider selection. I'll be open to fair offers, whether money or some sort of

exchange of goods. Thank you for your time, and I look forward to seeing you after the show. God bless you all.'

Abraham and his friends lead the donkeys out through the back door. The audience applaud politely.

MIKE: Well, there you go, folks. Abraham and his donkeys! Actually, just before we continue with the show, could I ask for someone to pop up here on stage and clear up some of this mess which the donkeys have kindly left! They're obviously healthy animals who eat well.

Luke, I'm so sorry. I've just noticed your sandals. You appear to have trodden in something the donkeys have left behind.

The audience find this very entertaining. The stage is cleaned up, and someone takes Luke's sandals to be cleaned.

LUKE: This is all great fun, Mike. If I have anything, it's a sense of humour. My sandals needed a good clean, anyway. It's not a problem.

MIKE: Like I said earlier, there's never a dull moment on this show. Could you just finish what you were explaining to us about the tax collectors, Samaritans and lepers?

LUKE: Certainly, Mike. The other group treated as outcasts by society and to whom Jesus showed love and compassion are those who suffer from that awful skin disease, leprosy. As you know, leprosy sufferers have to follow many rules and regulations. They have to stay away from other people, and if anyone accidentally approaches a leper, the leper has to shout out, 'Unclean, unclean!' This isn't just because they might spread the disease, but because lepers are also seen as spiritually unclean. They are not allowed to enter any place of worship. This explains what I wrote in my Gospel, chapter 5 verses 12 to 16, where a leper throws himself in front of

Jesus and shouts, 'If you want to, you can make me clean.' The wonderful part about this miracle, where Jesus healed the leper, is that he *touched* the man. You have to think hard what effect this would have had on that man. He may not have had any human contact for years, and yet Jesus touched him. This touch would have made Jesus unclean in the eyes of the Law, but his great power healed and cleansed the leper.

MIKE: That's a perfect example of Jesus' real love and compassion for those afflicted with this condition. I have already said that in today's show we have some folk with us who have leprosy, and many of you here have made them feel really welcome. After the show we are going to have a prayer meeting here, where we will ask the Lord to bless and heal our brothers and sisters suffering from leprosy. Luke has told me that he would love to be part of the meeting as well and he'll pray for them and lay his hands on them. God bless you, Luke, and may the peace of God be with our special guests at the back today.

The audience applaud. Many of them look round at the lepers and smile. Some give them a friendly wave.

Now, Luke, next week on the show I'll be chatting to John, and the following week my guest will be Paul.

As soon as Mike mentions the name 'Paul', a few of the women in the audience shout 'Boo'.

That's exactly the reaction I wanted. I know, when Paul comes on to the show, he's going to have a lot of explaining to do to the women in the audience. This brings me nicely on to my next point, Luke— women! As you know, religious teachers are encouraged not to teach or even speak with women. Some teachings state that a man must not talk to a woman in the street, not even to his own wife! I will discuss these issues with Paul in a couple of weeks, but what I'd like to ask you, Luke, is how Jesus treated women, bearing in mind that he was a religious teacher?

LUKE: Very simply, Mike, Jesus considered women on an equal plane with men.

A big cheer from all the women in the audience.

We can see this straight away from the way he taught women. In my Gospel, chapter 10 verses 38 to 42, I describe Jesus visiting the home of Martha and Mary. Martha was busy with housework, the so-called 'women's work'. Mary, however, took the 'male' role, sitting at the feet of Jesus and listening to his teaching. Martha thought that Mary was completely wrong to choose the role of some sort of intellectual, and so she complained to Jesus, saying, 'Lord, don't you care that my sister has left me to do all the work by myself? Please tell her to come and help me now!' Jesus' response was wonderful. He told Martha that she was troubled over so many things, and that in fact only one thing was important. Mary had chosen that one important thing, and in no way should it be taken away from her. She had chosen to study theology rather than be preoccupied with domestic chores.

Jesus refused to force women into stereotypes. Mary was treated as a person. Wanting to learn and understand Jesus' teaching was far more important than cleaning and cooking!

Audience really applaud at this point, especially the women!

MIKE: Also, in chapter 7 verses 36 to 50, you describe Jesus showing his compassion for women, when he visits the home of Simon the Pharisee.

LUKE: That's another perfect example of Jesus' remarkable attitude towards women—simply treating them as people and as equals. Simon would have been shocked to see any woman come in and touch Jesus, but this was a woman who had lived a 'sinful life', and here she was kissing and anointing his feet. How could Jesus be a real prophet and allow this behaviour? Well, this was Jesus, the Son of God, and this was his attitude towards women. If we claim to be followers of Jesus, then quite simply we have to follow his example.

Someone shouts out from the audience, 'You were a companion of Paul on his journeys. Why do his views on women seem to differ totally from your views and from what Jesus seems to be teaching? Who are we supposed to believe?'

MIKE: First of all, could I ask people not just to shout out? I do give folk a chance to ask questions throughout the show. I would like, however, to ask Luke to answer that question, as I'm sure it's one that many of us are thinking as we listen. Luke, what you say sounds so clear, but Paul is known to have written things like, 'Wives, submit yourselves to your husbands',[30] and 'It is a disgraceful thing for a woman to ever speak in church.'[31] What are we to make of all this? What did Paul mean?

LUKE: Mike, I think it's only fair that Paul should answer these questions himself in a couple of weeks' time. I would hate to sit here and say, 'This is what Paul meant.' All I can really say today is that Paul truly is a great man. Reading some of his letters and listening to what he teaches about women, you may think that he is contradicting Jesus' attitude towards women, and I can understand why many of the women hissed and booed at the mention of Paul's name earlier in the show. In Paul's defence, though, he also wrote the following in his letter to the Galatians: 'There is no difference between the Jews and Gentiles, between slaves and free people or between men and women. You are all one in union with Christ Jesus.'[32] Here, Paul seems to be quite clear that men and women are equal, so I think it's only fair that he should explain his views when he appears on the show. Like I say, he is a great man and a good friend, so please give him a chance to explain himself!

MIKE: I think that's fair enough. We certainly can't wait to have Paul on the show, and I'm sure the women will have plenty to ask him!

Big cheer from many of the women in the audience.

It really is an issue we could discuss for hours, but as far as Luke and the message in his Gospel is concerned, Jesus seems to make it quite clear that the idea that women are second-class citizens, inferior to men, should be unacceptable to any Christian.

I can't wait for you to look at my tooth after the show, Luke. It's very painful at the moment.

LUKE: If you could arrange for a cup of wine mixed with myrrh to be brought in now, I think you should drink it. Hopefully, within a while, the pain should lessen a little, and by the end of the show, I can pull the tooth out for you.

Somebody working backstage brings a glass to Mike. He drinks the solution fairly quickly, as the taste is awful. Myrrh is very bitter.

MIKE: Thanks, Luke. I hope that does the trick. One question I meant to ask you right at the start is the obvious one—why did you write your Gospel in the first place?

LUKE: As someone who was lucky enough to receive a good education, Mike, I simply wanted to write an account of Jesus' life that was historically accurate. That's why I mention the fact that I did check the information of eyewitnesses. Also, being a Gentile, my Gospel was largely aimed at educated Gentiles. The main message I wanted to get across is that Jesus is for everyone. He may have been the expected Jewish Messiah, but his ministry was not confined only to the Jews.

MIKE: I have to say, Luke, your Gospel really is well written. As you write in verse three of your first chapter, it's quite clear that you have 'carefully studied all these matters from the beginning'. The Gentile emphasis is also there from the beginning as you are writing to Theophilus, a high-ranking government official who was himself a Gentile Christian.

LUKE: Yes, my dear friend Theophilus. He paid for all the parchment I used, and he does a great deal for the Church, helping to spread the good news using what I wrote to him.

MIKE: Now then, Luke, what is unique about you is that you have written a second part to your Gospel. Again, this second book is written to Theophilus. What's it all about?

LUKE: As you say, Mike, I basically wrote a two-book set. My second book continues the story after the ascension of Jesus, looking at the life of the early Church. Quite simply, Mike (and not because I think you're simple)… *(audience laugh),* once you've finished reading the 24th chapter in my Gospel, you can just carry straight on with chapter 2 of my second book.

MIKE: That sounds simple enough to me. In your second book, you focus on the acts of those two great apostles Peter and Paul, so why not call your second book 'The Acts of the Apostles'?

LUKE: Love the idea!

Audience applaud.

MIKE: Nice name for a book, I think. Luke, I say this to all my guests: we only have a certain amount of time on the show, so we'll get straight down to some questions about your second book, the Acts of the Apostles. I've had loads of letters come in with questions for you, so here are some of the main ones that have been asked.

The first question that many folk want to put to you is 'Why in the book of Acts, chapter 16 verse 10, do you suddenly start to use the word "we"?'

LUKE: That's a very good question, and well spotted. You'll notice, if you read that part of my book, that I first write 'we' when Paul is off to Troas. He was on his second missionary journey, and it was at Troas that I joined him. I spent a fair bit of my time travelling around spreading the good news of Jesus, as well as helping sick people. I'd heard that Paul hadn't been feeling too good, so I arranged to meet up with him in Troas to see if I could help him medically, as well as with his mission. That's why, when I'm reporting this event in Paul's life, I write 'we', for the simple fact that I was there with him.

MIKE: Could you tell us what was medically wrong with Paul?

LUKE: I'm afraid that's something I can't do, Mike. There's got to be confidentiality between a doctor and his patient.

MIKE: No wonder Paul called you his beloved physician—a doctor you can really trust!

What can you tell us about the man Paul? Of course this is your show, Luke, and I'll be chatting to Paul soon, but just a brief word, if you don't mind.

LUKE: Trying to sum up Paul in just a brief word, Mike, is pretty much impossible. Where does one begin? He's an amazing man, and you'll all realize this when he comes to be a guest on your show. I'm sure the women will come to accept him as well; whatever he writes about women in his letters, I'm sure he'll explain himself.

'I hope so!' shouts a woman from the back.

I can tell you now what an educated man he is. Quite often, when I chatted to Paul—and you can also see this in his letters—he showed a keen knowledge of Greek rhetoric. He told me that he learned this in Tarsus. He also told me about the formal training he had in the Jewish Law when preparing to become a rabbi, and his teacher in Jerusalem was no less than Gamaliel!

Some of the audience members look impressed with this. Gamaliel was a very famous teacher.

MIKE: I was told that, in his letters to the Galatians[33] and the Philippians,[34] he wrote that he excelled in the study of the Law. I'm already building up this picture of a highly intelligent man. I hope that my questions to him won't seem too trivial.

LUKE: All I can say to that, Mike, is that despite this amazing background, he is really easy to chat to. He truly was a changed man after his conversion, and no doubt you'll be talking about that incident in your show. It's an amazing story—a miracle.

MIKE: I hope you don't mind me asking, but does Paul tend to 'go on' a little sometimes?

LUKE: Ah! I know where you're going with this question. When you ask whether Paul 'goes on' a little, do you mean 'Does he send people to sleep?'

MIKE: That's it, Luke. I'm referring to the story you tell in Acts 20 verses 7 to 12. You must have been there, as you write 'we' in the narrative. Tell us what happened.

LUKE: I knew this was the story you were talking about—the chap called Eutychus who fell asleep while Paul was preaching. I can tell you right now, Mike, that Paul never 'goes on'. On your show in a couple of weeks' time, you'll just want to chat to him for ever. I think you have misunderstood my account. Eutychus did not fall asleep because Paul was boring him to death! Let me explain what happened.

It was during Paul's last visit to Troas, a Saturday evening, and a group of us gathered together with Paul for the fellowship meal. After eating, Paul chatted to us all evening, until midnight. We knew he was leaving the next day, so we really wanted to hear his words. I have to tell you, Mike, it was stifling in the room and quite smoky, as we had many lamps burning. Our young friend Eutychus was so hot that he was sitting on the windowsill. The poor lad got a little sleepy and dozed off. It was nothing to do with Paul's words, as he was fascinating to listen to, as always. It was just the heat and smoke.

It might sound a little funny now, but when Eutychus dozed off, he fell out of the window!

Some of the audience giggle.

We were actually on the third storey and he fell to the ground. I was there and I could tell with my medical training that he was most certainly dead. I suspected that he had broken his neck. It was awful. Some of us got into a bit of a state, but Paul remained totally calm. He just fell to his knees, reached out to Eutychus and hugged him. He looked at us all and told us not to worry, that Eutychus was alive. As soon as he said this, Eutychus stood up! We were amazed. We all went back upstairs and carried on with the meal, making sure Eutychus sat well away from the window!

Audience laugh.

We carried on talking until sunrise, and then Paul had to leave. Eutychus went home; he was fit and well. We all felt full of the Holy Spirit. It had been a wonderful night, despite the accident.

MIKE: What an incredible story. I may try to get Eutychus to come on the show at some stage; it would be great to hear his side of events.

Now, we are well into the second half of today's show, slowly coming towards the end.

'No!' shout many members of the audience.

I'm afraid so, folks. I know that many of you are dying to chat to Luke and ask him questions, so if you don't mind, Luke, could we finish with some questions from the audience?

LUKE: I'd love to talk with any members of your audience, Mike.

MIKE: God bless you, Luke! Would anyone out there like to ask something?

Loads of hands shoot up into the air.

MIKE: Let's go for the man over there with plenty of beard but not so much on top; yes, you, sir. What's your name, where are you from, and what's your question for Luke?

'I presume I'm the baldy you're talking about! My name is Solomon and I'm from Jerusalem. A friend of mine recently described your Gospel, Luke, as the "great Gospel of forgiveness". What's your reaction to that?'

LUKE: I'm so glad your friend described my Gospel like that, Solomon. A key aim of mine was to put across the great importance of forgiveness. Forgiveness was central to the whole of Jesus' ministry. I don't know whether you have noticed, but I include many episodes and parables in my Gospel that you won't find in Matthew's or Mark's Gospels, and these extra bits all deal with this issue of forgiveness.

MIKE: Could you give us some examples, Luke?

LUKE: For a start, there are those wonderful parables of forgiveness —the lost sheep, the lost coin and, of course, the prodigal son. These are in chapter 15 of my Gospel. There is also that lovely moment that I mention in chapter 19, involving the chief tax collector Zacchaeus. Zacchaeus was a tiny little man, and one day, when Jesus was passing through Jericho, he wanted to see this teacher that everybody was talking about. Because he was so small, he had to climb up a sycamore tree to see over the crowd!

Quite a few of the audience smile at this story.

Jesus looked up and saw him there, and I can imagine he must have laughed to himself as well. He told Zacchaeus to get down because he wanted to stay in his house. Zacchaeus was delighted. It reminds me of how Matthew described on your show how he felt when Jesus first spoke to him. When Jesus said he wanted to stay at Zacchaeus' house, the crowd started complaining, saying, 'How can Jesus stay in the house of this terrible sinner?'

Then Zacchaeus stood up and shouted, 'I'll give half my belongings to the poor, and if I've cheated anyone, I'll pay them back four times as much.' Jesus told the crowd that salvation had come to Zacchaeus' house that day and that he too was a descendant of Abraham—a man with real faith and understanding. Jesus concluded by saying, 'The Son of Man has come to seek and save the lost.'

MIKE: I love that story. You know, I met Zacchaeus recently; he's a really lovely chap. He's out of the tax collecting business now, and busy doing the Lord's work. He may be a little man, but he has a huge heart, full of love and compassion. God bless him!

Talking of forgiveness, Luke, there is also that most awful event when Jesus really practised what he preached—forgiving others for their terrible cruelty to him.

LUKE: Yes, Jesus had just been brutally nailed to the cross, and he was still able to say, 'Father, forgive them! They do not know what they are doing.'[35] If my Gospel has to be called the Gospel of forgiveness, this moment in Jesus' life has to be the ultimate example of forgiveness being shown, to an amazing extent.

MIKE: Thanks, Luke, and thank you, Solomon, for the question. Could we have another question, please? The lady towards the back in the blue robe; yes, you, madam.

'Hi. My name is Ruth. I'm from Bethany. I am the mother of four children, and my question relates to Mary as the mother of Jesus. From what you know, Luke, what on earth was it really like for Mary—the angel, the virgin birth, the young boy Jesus in the temple?'

MIKE: Wow! What a question! This reminds me, Luke, you're the only Gospel writer who mentions anything about the childhood of Jesus, or the 'hidden years', as I've heard some call them. Great question, Ruth! Tell us about Mary, Luke.

LUKE: Mary was only about fifteen years old when the angel Gabriel first spoke to her. Can you imagine it? The poor girl was quite terrified. Having an angel come to visit you is frightening enough, but what Gabriel had to say to Mary was quite staggering. 'You will become pregnant and give birth to a Son, and you'll name him Jesus.'[36] I had the wonderful honour of meeting Mary, and, like Ruth, I too was very interested in what the experience was like for her. Despite the most awful shock of the angel's visit and the disturbing news about giving birth to a son, she was able to accept this message humbly, simply because her faith was so strong. I'm sure I don't need to remind you about the dreadful disgrace this news would bring on her, an unmarried, pregnant girl. Mary told me that she was very frightened. Who wouldn't be? But I can tell you now, Mary is an amazing woman, and it's quite clear to me why God chose her to give birth to Jesus.

Her next big worry was having to tell Joseph about her pregnancy. I'm not surprised! Not many men would say to their bride-to-be, 'No problems, darling! I understand', having just heard that an angel had told her she was going to have a baby.

Audience laugh.

73

Mary actually went to visit her relative Elizabeth, who was a great help to her. Elizabeth told her that this was God's work and that he would sort it all out, and that Joseph would come to understand—which he did, thanks to another visit from an angel. In fact, Matthew deals with Joseph's side of the story, if you want to read it. It was while Mary was at Elizabeth's that she truly demonstrated her great faith, praising God for choosing her to do this wonderful thing.

MIKE: Luke, there's a verse in chapter 2 of your Gospel which I'd like you to explain. It's verse 19. Basically, Mary had given birth and the shepherds had come to visit the baby. They tell Mary about their experience in the field with the angel, and the great army of angels that had appeared, singing and praising God. You write, 'Mary remembered all these things and thought about them deeply.' What was going through her mind?

LUKE: Here we have a fifteen-year-old girl. An angel visits her, telling her she's to give birth to God's son. She has the baby in a stable, of all places, and then shepherds come to visit her, talking about more angels. What an amazing train of events to happen to a young girl! Mary told me that not a moment went by when she didn't want just to sit and think over all these extraordinary happenings. A miracle of miracles! Of course she would remember all these things and think deeply about them.

Then there was that occasion when Jesus was twelve years old, when he went with Mary and Joseph to Jerusalem for the Passover festival. When it was time to go home, Jesus stayed in Jerusalem, but his parents didn't know this. They assumed at first that he was in the big crowd, somewhere, who were all on the way home. Three days later, having returned to Jerusalem, they found him in the temple, sitting with the Jewish teachers, listening to them and asking questions. Everyone was astonished at how intelligent he was, and at how he gave such thoughtful answers.

When Mary told me this story, she said that, like any mother—and I'm sure Ruth would understand this—she was extremely worried, and she told Jesus that she and Joseph had been desperately searching for him. It was then that Jesus gave his amazing reply: 'Why have you been looking for me? Didn't you know that I'd be in my Father's house?'[37] It's a terrible thing for any parent to realize that they don't understand their own child, but this is exactly what happened. Mary had actually found Jesus at work. He was not only her son, but also the heavenly Father's Son, sent on a mission in which she now found him totally involved. Mary was sad. Jesus had said, 'my Father', and up to this time Joseph had always been known by that title. Like any mother would, Mary felt that this was the first time when she sensed a separation between herself and Jesus.

But as time went by, she did come to understand what was happening, and as she told me, she 'treasured all these things in her heart'.

MIKE: What a great question, Ruth, and thank you, Luke, for giving us such a wonderful insight into Mary, the mother of Jesus.

We have definitely got time for one more question from the audience. The gentleman in the third row in the purple; yes, you, sir.

'Hello, Luke. I notice in your Gospel, in chapter 4, you tell us about Jesus in the desert being tempted by Satan. I don't mean to appear ignorant, but what were these temptations all about? I thought temptations were supposed to be bad things, but what was bad about Jesus' temptations? Turning stones into bread seems pretty OK to me if you haven't eaten for forty days! Could you please explain them?'

MIKE: Sorry, what is your name, sir?

'My name is Joseph, from Jerusalem.'

MIKE: You know, Joseph, just to make you feel better, I've never really understood what was going on with those temptations either. Hope you don't think we're daft, Luke, but I really look forward to hearing what you have to say about them.

LUKE: Of course I don't think either of you is daft! Not a day goes by when I'm not explaining the temptations of Jesus to someone.

To get things into context, just before his time of temptation, Jesus had been baptized, which was an overwhelming religious experience. He clearly understood that he was the long-awaited Messiah, and he needed to be alone to contemplate and pray, to work out and understand how he was to fulfil this role. Where quieter to go than the desert, a place of complete silence? It was after forty days without food in the desert that Jesus was tempted. He was obviously starving, weak with hunger. Why not turn some stones into bread?

Jesus knew that, just as Moses fed the people with manna in the wilderness,[38] perhaps the Messiah should produce 'bread from heaven'. This would be a great way to feed all the starving in Palestine! But when Jesus was tempted to do this miracle, he replied, 'Man shall not live by bread alone.'[39]

MIKE: So why did Jesus reject this temptation?

LUKE: For the simple reason that he didn't want to use his power for selfish reasons. Also, Jesus had come to feed people's souls, not their bellies! They had spiritual as well as physical needs. If Jesus went around turning stones into bread, the people would start expecting him to do that all the time. This was not why Jesus came into the world. He was here to lead people to God.

MIKE: Well, well! That explains it so clearly. Thank you, Luke. What about the second temptation, the promise of worldly power?

LUKE: Remember, Mike, the Jews were expecting a political Messiah —a man like King David who would defeat their enemies. Jesus must have wondered in the desert whether this was the way to fulfil his role as Messiah. Should he go to war and use violence to destroy Israel's enemies?

But Jesus could never do things that way. It would have been the devil's way. It is through peace, joy and love that God's kingdom will be established, not through war, violence and force. This is why Jesus rejected this temptation, saying, 'Worship the Lord your God and serve only him.' [40]

The final temptation was when Jesus imagined himself on the pinnacle of the temple, and the devil asked him to jump off. The devil said that Jesus need not worry because the angels would make sure he didn't get hurt. Now, Jesus would certainly have known the prophecy in Malachi 3 verse 1 of the Messiah 'suddenly' coming to his temple. If Jesus had jumped off the top of the temple, it would certainly have been seen as a fulfilment of this prophecy. Also, if he had jumped off and floated down, it would have been a real crowd puller! Very tempting!

But Jesus wasn't having any of this. Real faith in God involves trusting him, not testing him—and people would soon have grown tired of tricks, jumping off temples and so on. This was not the way to win people to God. This is why Jesus says in chapter 4 verse 12, 'You shall not put the Lord God to the test.'

The audience give Luke a huge round of applause for his clear explanation of the temptations of Jesus.

MIKE: Luke, thank you so much for that. I'm sure Joseph is very happy with that response. I know it all makes more sense to me now.

You know, that devil was very sneaky, wasn't he, quoting from scripture to tempt Jesus?

LUKE: That's right, Mike. In the last temptation, the devil said to Jesus, 'Throw yourself down from here *because the scripture says*, "God will order his angels to take good care of you."' Very sneaky indeed, and of course the devil did this for his own ends. But Jesus rejected each temptation by quoting scripture, which is of course the word of God. By doing this, he put himself under God's authority.

MIKE: I'm afraid, everybody, that by looking at the long shadows in the courtyard here, I see we really are at the end of the show. What an excellent New Testament writer we've had on the show this evening—the people's writer!

Big cheers from the audience.

Thank you so much for coming in to chat to us, Luke. You've been a real star, and we've learned so much from you.

LUKE: The pleasure has been all mine. Now let's get that tooth sorted out for you, and then I look forward to taking part in the prayer and healing meeting after the show.

MIKE: Just before I lose a tooth, a reminder that next week on the show, I'll be chatting to someone a little different, and no doubt quite fascinating. Matthew's, Mark's and Luke's Gospels are pretty similar, on the whole, but John's is a whole different ball game—whatever that means—and talking to him will be most interesting. Join me next week for *So you think you're a New Testament writer*.

---

25 Colossians 4:14.

26 Luke 1:53.

27 Luke 4:18.

28 Luke was born a slave in Antioch, Syria, and studied to become a physician. It was common for slaves to become the doctor of the family unit that owned them.

29 This was an ethnic group related to the Jewish people, who, as a result of marrying non-Jews, became figures of hatred.

30 Ephesians 5:22.

31 1 Corinthians 14:35.

32 Galatians 3:28.

33 Galatians 1:14.

34 Philippians 3:6.

35 Luke 23:34.

36 Luke 1:31.

37 Luke 2:49.

38 Exodus 16.

39 Luke 4:4.

40 Luke 4:8.

Mike Coles chats to John

MUSICAL INTRODUCTION

A large group of men and women walk on to the stage. They sing a hymn, the words of which are recorded in Paul's letter to the Philippians, chapter 2 verses 5 to 11. It's a rousing hymn, and many of the audience stand and join in. They sing it at least three times! At the end, the choir are applauded. Then Mike begins the show.

MIKE: Ladies and gentlemen, it's great to see you all here this evening for another edition of *So you think you're a New Testament writer*.

Before I introduce you to this week's guest, can I just thank all those who have been asking after my tooth! I have to say that Luke did a wonderful job, although I needed a fair bit of wine first! From now on, I shall also refer to Luke as my 'beloved physician'.

Well, tonight's special guest was once just an ordinary fisherman with his brother James. Their father was Zebedee. They were both called by Jesus to be disciples, and he actually nicknamed them 'the sons of thunder'. Sadly, King Herod Agrippa I had James executed, and his brother has recently been exiled on the island of Patmos, thanks to the Emperor Domitian! Well, we've managed to sneak him away from there, and straight after the show we're going to help him get to Ephesus, where he'd like to live his last days in peace. Ladies and gentlemen, will you please give a huge, warm welcome to John!

The audience burst into deafening applause, many of them clearly amazed to see him brought back from exile.

John comes on stage fairly slowly; he's reached a great age, but there is still plenty of life in him. Before he reaches Mike, he stops and looks at the audience, giving them an enthusiastic wave and warm smile.

MIKE: John, welcome to the show. I hardly know where to begin. Once a fisherman, then a disciple of Jesus—and not just any old disciple, but possibly the closest of all the disciples to Jesus. You've written a Gospel and some letters. You were exiled to the island of Patmos, and just before the show you were telling me about the most amazing revelation you've had from God—a series of bizarre visions! Ladies and gentlemen, John has promised me that in today's show he will tell us about some of those revelations. We will be the first to hear about them before he writes them down as a book. John, welcome.

JOHN: Thank you, Mike.

MIKE: I think I'd like to begin the show as I did with Matthew, and ask you about your first encounter with Jesus, when he called you to be his disciple. How did it happen?

JOHN: Well, as you know, I was a fisherman with my brother James. We had often seen and heard Jesus preaching beside the lake. This man was different from other teachers. He spoke with such authority. His words would echo in my mind for weeks and weeks. James and I realized quite soon that this man spoke the truth. That moment when he asked James and me to follow him was truly amazing. We had talked and talked about this man Jesus. When he asked us to follow him, it seemed so natural to say yes. We wanted to know and learn so much more from him.

MIKE: You and your brother were given a nickname by Jesus. How did that come about?

JOHN: It's quite a funny story, as it happens. The day that Jesus asked us to be his disciples, we were just coming back from a fishing trip. We had had a poor catch. James and I were having a huge argument. I had suggested to James that we fish in a certain part of the lake that day, but he'd steered us somewhere else. I blamed the poor catch on him. We argued and shouted about it all the way back to the shore. We didn't realize it at the time, but Jesus was standing there listening with a smile on his face. He found the whole incident quite amusing. The first thing he said to us as we stepped out of the boat was 'Boanerges!'[41] which, as you know, means 'men of thunder'. James and I looked at each other and burst out laughing. Jesus smiled at us and then said, 'Follow me.' I remember just glancing at James. We both nodded to each other. We were sure it was the right decision.

I knew at that moment that my whole life was to change. In a split second I had decided to give up my whole livelihood, my family ties, everything, to follow this man Jesus. But it felt so right.

MIKE: You were telling me before the show that this is often how Jesus calls people to follow him. The call can come in the middle of your everyday work.

JOHN: That's right, Mike. God's call is not confined to 'holy' people in holy, religious places. The other thing about being called to follow Jesus—whether then, now or in the future—is that it does require sacrificing something. Simon and Andrew had to give up their job and way of life, as did James and I. We also had to give up our family ties.

MIKE: I suppose that's the same with discipleship at any time—the fact that it involves some sort of sacrifice.

Now, John, it doesn't take much to work out that your Gospel is very different from the other three. Many people refer to the other three as the 'synoptic' Gospels, as they are all so similar, using similar sources and so on. But your Gospel is nothing like them! I mean, you hardly mention any miracles—and where have all the parables gone?

Many of the audience titter at Mike's humorous tone.

You also include long speeches that Jesus gives, instead of the lovely little sayings that the synoptic Gospels present. In your Gospel you also show Jesus talking a lot more about himself, and he seems to spend a lot more time in Jerusalem. Why so different, John?

JOHN: In my Gospel, chapter 20 verse 31, I set out the reason why I wrote it. The purpose of my Gospel is that you 'may believe that Jesus is the Messiah, the Son of God. If you have faith in him you will have life.'

How is this any different from the other three Gospels? All four have this simple message. In this sense, my Gospel is similar to the others.

The audience applaud. They love John's response to Mike's question.

MIKE: Great answer, John. That really shut me up.

Audience laugh.

JOHN: I believe I understand the point you were really getting at, though, Mike. All the Gospels have their own style. Matthew has a 'Jewish' touch to his Gospel, always quoting from scripture to show how prophecies have been fulfilled. Luke, the educated man, gives us a very accurate and well-researched account. Mark's Gospel, as we know, is the 'action-packed' Gospel, full of energy.

All around me, there has always been an atmosphere of Gnosticism,[42] and I think this has affected my style of thought and writing.

MIKE: You know, I heard someone say the other day that, in a way, you have translated the good news into Greek philosophy! Some other chap recently told me that the way you present Jesus in your Gospel is like 'a riddle wrapped in a mystery inside an enigma'.[43]

Audience laugh.

JOHN: That's a clever way of putting it. I don't think that was my intention, but I was aware that the style of my Gospel might appeal particularly to many of the Hellenists[44] around, as well as to people generally.

MIKE: Those Gnostics have certainly influenced you a little as well. Something quite common to Gnostic thought is the whole idea of dualism—in other words, a load of symbolic opposites. Could you explain some of these 'opposites' that you use in your Gospel, John?

JOHN: Quite simply, Mike, the dualistic ideas I use in my Gospel are life and death; light and darkness; God and Satan; spirit and flesh; above and below; heaven and earth; truth and falsehood; (true) Israel and 'the Jews'; belief and unbelief.

Just to give you an example, we could say that this world has become totally corrupted by Satan, as I write in chapter 12 verse 31. In other words, we are in 'darkness'.[45] The world needs saving. God did this by sending his son, the light of the world, into the darkness. I write in chapter 3 verse 16, 'God loved the world so much that he gave his only Son, so that all who believe in him may not die but have eternal life.'

I must make it clear, though, that in no way do I endorse the Gnostics' perspective. I simply use some of their terms to help me communicate with my audience.

MIKE: I often hear people quoting that verse, John. In fact, there are some folk sat in the audience today with some placards; could all those with placards please hold them up?

Many of the audience hold up their placards. On all of them is written, 'John 3:16'!

There you go, John. I didn't ask them to do this. It's such a powerful message; it sums up the whole Gospel. I think this idea of writing

'John 3:16' on placards at big public meetings or events might catch on, you know.

JOHN: I love it! A great way to spread the message!

MIKE: We've already touched on Gnosticism, dualistic thought and so on, so we don't want to continue too much with all this 'heavy' talk.

Audience laugh.

But I would like to focus briefly on chapter 1 of your Gospel and discuss the '*logos*'[46] Before we chat about this, John, could you just read us the first five verses of chapter 1 from your Gospel, so that we can hear what you write about 'the Word'?

JOHN: 'Before the world was created, the Word already existed. He was with God, and was the same as God. The Word was with God from the very beginning. Through him God made everything; not one thing in creation was made without him. The Word was the source of life, and this life brought life to all humankind. The light shines in the darkness, and the darkness has never put it out.'[47]

MIKE: We can see some dualism at work again in that short passage —the light and darkness. Now, John, could you talk us through this idea of the *logos*, the Word, just to explain it to some of us, including me? It's certainly a different style of writing and thought, compared to the other Gospel writers.

JOHN: Well done for spotting the dualism in those few verses, Mike. This whole idea about the *logos* or Word is not actually mine. The idea is from a Jewish-Hellenistic hymn. Of course, being Jewish, the hymn is not referring to a pre-existent divine 'Son', Jesus, but it's about God and his *logos*, his Word—in other words, his Wisdom in creating the world.

When I wrote the prologue to my Gospel, I didn't change the words of this hymn, which said that the Word was with God from the beginning. What I did was to give it a Christian meaning, by adding 'the Word became flesh, full of truth, and lived among us.'[48] This is the key verse in my prologue. God's Word is the light and life of us all. God's Word was there at creation and is at work everywhere. The wonderful thing now is that the Word came into the world. We saw the Word; he came to live with us as one of us. Praise God!

The audience give John a huge round of applause for his beautiful explanation of what is sometimes a tricky passage to understand.

MIKE: So, Jesus of Nazareth is the Word made flesh. He is God's *logos* in person or, I suppose you could say, God's wisdom in human form.

JOHN: Well done, Mike! I think you are beginning to understand how to use this more philosophical way of expressing yourself. I write like this because I've grown up listening to people all around me talking in this way. If I'm to communicate the gospel to them, I need to write in a way that will mean something to them.

MIKE: I like it when people tell me I'm beginning to understand things! Thanks, John.

OK, folks. It's that time of the show when I like to ask members of the audience if they have a question for our special guest. Let's start with the man on the far left-hand side—the chap with the huge beard!

'Hi, my name's Nathan. I'm from Capernaum. I'd just like to say, it's great to see you here today, John. We all know you were sent to Patmos for preaching the good news. God bless you.'

The audience applaud.

'John, I think among the most distinctive features of your Gospel are the "I am" sayings of Jesus. Could you tell us more about them?'

JOHN: Hello, Nathan, and thank you for your kind words. There were seven times when Jesus openly declared who he was, and each time those declarations began with the words 'I am'. The first of these sayings can be found in chapter 6 of my Gospel, verse 35. Jesus says, 'I am the bread of life. He who comes to me will never hunger, and he who believes in me will never thirst.' What is interesting about all these sayings is that they pick up some key themes from the Old Testament—such as Moses being the giver of manna, the bread from heaven, Israel as the vine or God as the shepherd of Israel—and then apply each one to Jesus.

Before I make my next point, Mike, answer me this question. How does God reveal himself to Moses in Exodus 3 verse 14?

MIKE: God said to Moses, 'I am who I am.'[49] Hey, John, I can see where you're going with this.

JOHN: Exactly, Mike! There is an amazing similarity between Jesus' 'I am' sayings and the words that God spoke to Moses at the burning bush. So by referring to himself as '*I am* the bread', or '*I am* the way', Jesus is telling us that he is God.

MIKE: John, you told us that there are seven of these 'I am' sayings; you've already mentioned one of them to us. What are the other six?

JOHN: In short, the seven are: I am 'the bread of life',[50] 'the light of the world',[51] 'the gate for the sheep',[52] 'the good shepherd',[53] 'the resurrection and the life',[54] 'the way, the truth, and the life',[55] and 'the true vine'.[56]

MIKE: To me, John, the most powerful one is Jesus saying he is 'the way, the truth, and the life'. Could you tell us a bit more about that saying?

JOHN: This one was actually an answer to a question. Jesus had been telling the disciples about the rooms in his Father's house and how he was going there to prepare a place for them. Thomas had asked, 'We don't know where you are going, Lord, so how do we know how to get there?'[57] It was then that Jesus answered Thomas, 'I am the way, the truth, and the life. Nobody can get to the Father except by me.'[58]

This is one of Jesus' supreme affirmations, probably the most fundamental idea in the whole of my Gospel. It is through Christ that we will know the Father—in other words, we will possess truth and life.

MIKE: One of the other 'I am' sayings is 'I am the resurrection and the life', which Jesus said before one of his most amazing miracles, the raising of Lazarus from the dead. I would love to chat to you about this miracle later in the show.

I'd like to go back to the audience now for another question. Let's have a look. OK, the lady in green sitting in the second row. What's your name and what's your question for John?

'Hello, Mike. Hello, John. My name is Bathsheba. I know you will like this question, Mike; it's to do with wine!'

MIKE: I don't know what you mean!

'You may have guessed already, but I'm referring to the wedding in Cana where John writes about Jesus' first miracle, turning water into wine. I have been talking to my friends about this and we really can't understand why the almighty power of God was used to solve such a small materialistic problem. Jesus turned six huge stone jars of water into good wine.[59] You have only chosen nine miracles to include in your Gospel, John, so you must have thought that this was an important one. My question to you is whether there was some deeper symbolic meaning behind this miracle, or was Jesus just a good chap to take to parties in case you ran out of drink?'

Audience laugh at the cheek of this question!

JOHN: Thank you for the question, Bathsheba. I suppose, when you compare this miracle with all the others I mention, and the miracles described in the other three Gospels, it certainly is a little different. Just to let you all know, I record this miracle at the wedding in Cana in chapter 2 of my Gospel, verses 1 to 12.

Now, of course, it was wonderful to be at this party and have someone produce nearly six huge stone jars full of really good wine because the host had miscalculated the amount to provide. Who wouldn't like to have someone like this come to a party with them? I know Mike would love it!

Audience laugh.

MIKE: Again, I don't know what you mean!

Audience laugh again.

JOHN: That's obviously the humorous side to the whole story. I remember clearly at the wedding how many people were totally amazed at this miracle, but also joking about it. Some were telling Jesus that they had parties planned in the near future, and could he come along, just in case! Jesus did see the funny side to this, as did all the disciples. It was such a happy occasion.

But Bathsheba asked me whether there was a more symbolic meaning behind this miracle. Most definitely! As I write in my Gospel, 'Jesus performed this first miracle in Cana in Galilee. It was here that he revealed his glory and his disciples believed in him.'[60] To begin with, this was a great miracle in which Jesus certainly did reveal his glory. From my own point of view, just witnessing this miracle gave me a deeper understanding of who this man Jesus truly was. Our faith was always strengthened when we witnessed him performing miracles.

Remember that Jesus was intent on fulfilling messianic prophecies. Isaiah predicted a ministry for the Messiah in Galilee[61]—Galilee, which had always been the first area to suffer grief and darkness as Babylon and Assyria and many others charged through to conquer Israel. Now Galilee would be the first to get the light of the gospel.

Another wonderful thing we learn from this miracle at Cana is that it demonstrates how Jesus was a Saviour for everyone, rich or poor. He went to parties; he mingled with everyone. We know that throughout his ministry he taught Pharisees, scribes, teachers of the Law, men and women, tax collectors and prostitutes. Jesus came to seek and save that which was lost.

Finally, I suppose the symbolic part of this miracle involves the water and the wine. As you know, the water in the stone jars would normally have been used for ritual washings.[62] But Jesus changed the water into wine, which is a symbol of his blood, and it is this that can truly wash away sin.

Many of the audience applaud here, as they are suddenly enlightened by the meaning of this miracle.

JOHN: You know that the master of the whole wedding feast said to Jesus about the wine, 'You have saved the best for last!'[63] This, of course, is also symbolic of Jesus' blood.

I would say to you, Bathsheba, and to all of you, next time you read this miracle or are discussing it, think how it should make us want to praise Jesus. We praise Jesus for being the Saviour of all. We praise him for his almighty power and great wisdom. But the greatest praise goes to him for shedding his blood, so that all of us might have our sins washed away.

Many of the audience members stand and shout 'Amen!' There is a great round of applause.

MIKE: Bathsheba, thanks for a great question. John, what a pleasure it is to have you here, giving such helpful and inspiring answers.

It's that time of the show where we have a little advert, and today's is actually linked to the miracle at the wedding in Cana. In a previous show, there was a lovely chap who just popped out of the audience and ran up to the stage and offered me some wine. His name was Jeremiah, and I've invited him back on the show to advertise his wine.

Jeremiah shouts out:

'FOR THE BEST WINE… TRY SOME OF MINE!'

'Hi. My name's Jeremiah. My wine may not be miraculous, but it's a wonderful drop. Mike will vouch for that! Whether it's for medicinal use, weddings, parties, or to remember our Lord's words and actions at his last supper, mine is the wine. Please see me after today's show for a free tasting and purchases.'

MIKE: Thanks very much, Jeremiah. I can certainly vouch for Jeremiah; his wine is perfect. I look forward to the free tasting after the show.

I mentioned a little earlier, John, that I'd like to chat to you about that amazing miracle, Lazarus being raised from the dead.[64] There's so much I'd like to ask you about it that I don't really know where to begin. I'd like to know what you saw and how you felt. Was there some purpose behind Lazarus being sick? When you heard about Lazarus' sickness, why didn't you rush to him straight away instead of delaying for two days? I think I'll stop there before I reel off thousands more questions!

JOHN: This miracle was so spiritually moving, Mike, it's almost impossible to put it into words. The awesome power of the Son of God was truly revealed on this day. Just to give you a little background, Lazarus was the brother of Mary and Martha. They were close friends of Jesus. Mary was the lady who poured perfume on Jesus' feet and wiped them with her hair. Lazarus and his sisters lived in Bethany, which, as you know, is just a couple of miles from Jerusalem.

What happened was that Mary and Martha sent some messengers to tell Jesus that Lazarus, his dear friend, was really ill. I was with Jesus when the news arrived. I didn't know what was wrong with Lazarus, but it sounded serious. I thought Jesus would immediately set off to Bethany. Instead he said, 'The end result of Lazarus' illness will not be death. This has happened to bring glory to God. It will be the means by which the Son of God will be glorified.'[65]

I didn't really have a clue what Jesus meant at that moment. It wasn't until I saw the unbelievable miracle that it all made sense to me. The sickness and death of Lazarus had a higher purpose. It was for the glory of God. When Lazarus came out of the tomb wrapped in grave-clothes, when I saw him raised to life, my faith and that of all the disciples was strengthened, as was the faith of many of the observers.

One of the points you raised, Mike, is why Jesus didn't go straight to Bethany when he'd heard about Lazarus' illness. I can tell you now, that certainly baffled us at the time. But again, it made sense once we'd witnessed the miracle. Jesus didn't delay because he didn't care or was too busy. He knew there was a more important purpose to Lazarus' sickness, and this took priority over Mary's and Martha's distress. How often in our lives do we want things to happen right here and now? We need to understand that the timing is in God's hands. We may feel sometimes that God does not care for us, but he really does. He will always help us in his time and in his way.

MIKE: That's such an important point! People often ask me, 'Why hasn't God answered my prayer?' But it's like you say—God will answer your prayers, but in his own way and time. Some chap summed it up perfectly when he told me that he'd been asking God for strength. What God actually gave him was a load of hardship, but it made him stronger. He'd also asked God for wisdom. What he actually got was a load of problems, which he then had to solve, and in so doing he became all the wiser. He concluded by telling me that he'd not received anything he'd asked for, but had received everything he really needed.

JOHN: Amazing! We got into all this just by talking about why Jesus didn't go to Bethany.

'Praise the Lord!' shout some of the audience.

MIKE: I've just thought, John. This 'raising from the dead' miracle is unique compared to the other similar miracles. Jesus had raised Jairus' daughter while her body was still in her father's house. He had also raised the widow of Nain's son while the body was being carried to the place of burial. But your account of the raising of Lazarus is the only time we read about Jesus resurrecting a body which had already been in the grave for four days and was in a state of decay.

JOHN: I know it's not pleasant to mention it, but when I saw Jesus perform this miracle, that's one of the first things I thought about. Even Martha said that there would be an awful smell when the stone was rolled away. As Jesus said, we were about to see God's glory, but I felt foolish standing there wondering how bad the smell was going to be.

It was at this point that Jesus shouted, 'Lazarus, come out!'[66] And I saw Lazarus standing there. His feet and hands were wrapped in grave-clothes, and he had a cloth around his face. I saw Mary and Martha run up to him and hug him. They were crying with joy and just wouldn't let him go.

'What more proof do I need?' I thought to myself. 'This man is the Son of God.' What Jesus had said to Martha made perfect sense: 'I am the resurrection, and the life. All those who believe in me, even though they are dead, will live.'[67]

MIKE: I can only begin to imagine what that must have been like, John. Thank you very much for sharing that with us.

Audience applaud.

Just before we leave this story, there's just one other point that interests me, and that's where you tell us that Jesus cried when Mary and the people with her were so upset at Lazarus' death. What did it mean to you to see Jesus, the Son of God, crying like that?

JOHN: I think that Mark deals with this whole issue very well—the fact that although Jesus is the Son of God, he was also fully human. Jesus ate with us, grew tired, and got annoyed with us for not understanding him half the time. He really did feel for Mary and Martha and all those who were devastated at the death of Lazarus, and was moved to tears.

MIKE: I've just noticed the shadows slowly creeping across the stage, which tells me that we don't have a huge amount of time left. But there is so much more I still want to talk about, including that very brief description from John about the amazing revelation he has had on the island of Patmos.

Before we chat about this revelation, John, some members of the audience grabbed me before the show and asked me if I could get you to talk briefly about your three letters. Could you sum up why you wrote them, and what the main message of these letters is?

JOHN: My first letter simply encourages Christians to love each other and God, and I also warn them to be aware of the enemies of the faith and their false teachings, which could destroy the Christian fellowship. My second letter basically has the same message, and this one I address to 'the dear lady' and 'her children', which was my way of saying a local church and her members.

MIKE: A sweet way of putting it!

JOHN: I thought so!

Audience laugh.

My third letter is to a man called Gaius, a church leader. I praise Gaius for all his hard work in helping other Christians. I also warn him about a proud leader called Diotrephes from a nearby church. That's pretty much it in a nutshell, Mike.

MIKE: That's great, John, thanks. Just one question on what you've said—what were the false teachings that you had to warn against?

JOHN: Some of the nonsense being taught was that everything physical is completely evil—the world, our bodies! The people teaching this went on to claim that Jesus couldn't have been really human, because how could God ever get physically involved with such an evil world? They also taught that we could do whatever we liked with our bodies because they were evil anyway.

I condemn this ridiculous teaching in my first letter by saying that Jesus was fully human. I had personally seen Jesus, listened to him and touched him. And we can't do whatever we want with our bodies. As Christians, we do what God wants because 'God is light, and there is no darkness at all in him'.[68]

Finally, in chapter 4 of my first letter, I encourage Christians to love one another because love comes from God. No one can ever say they love God if they actually hate other people. Being a Christian means truly loving others and demonstrating this love in everything we do and say.

'Amen to that!' many folk shout out from the audience.

MIKE: It's a real shame that we have hardly any time left. It feels as if we've only just started and there's so much more I'd love to chat about. To finish tonight's show, I'd like to ask you a couple more questions, John. Before I ask you briefly to share with us what happened on Patmos, could you tell us why in your Gospel you describe yourself as the 'disciple whom Jesus loved'?

JOHN: It is a shame that the show's coming to an end. I've enjoyed chatting to you, and the audience has been great!

The audience cheer and give John a big round of applause.

Do you know what it's like when you just 'click' with someone instantly? That's exactly how it was like with me and Jesus, from the very first moment he spoke to me and gave my brother and me that daft nickname, 'men of thunder'. My brother and I were really fiery characters, and this always amused Jesus. From the very beginning we felt close to him. It was always me, James and Peter who were with Jesus on important occasions—such as when he raised Jairus's daughter.[69] There was also the occasion when Jesus was transfigured,[70] and that awful evening when he prayed before his arrest and death.[71]

I felt so close to Jesus. There were many times when he told me how much he loved me, and what a true and faithful disciple I was. It was because of this very special bond that I used the words 'the disciple whom Jesus loved' in my Gospel.

MIKE: And we are so honoured to have you here today, John. Just before the end, could you please tell us a bit about your amazing experience on Patmos—the 'revelation' you received?

JOHN: You know, Mike, I had been wondering for quite a while whether I should tell anybody about this revelation. I didn't want people to be confused by it, or to see things in the revelation that aren't actually there. But I have decided that I will write it down for all to read, and I will briefly tell you about it today.

What you need to realize is how terribly the Romans are persecuting us at the moment. No Christian will ever bow down and worship the Emperor Domitian. Because of this, we are being seen as traitors and put to death.

I know that many Christians are wondering why evil seems to be triumphing at the moment. What's going to happen to us? Will we survive? Will God ever help us?

The wonderful revelation I had on Patmos was an answer to all these questions. Many of the visions I had were totally bizarre, the same sort of visions you might find in the writings of Daniel or Zechariah. When you eventually get to read my book of Revelation, the main point I will be making is that there is a God who rules over everything. In my visions I saw a huge battle between the forces of good and evil. As Christians, we should never be in any doubt that God will defeat the devil. Rome may be exerting its power against us at the moment, but this power is weak and pathetic compared to the mighty power of our God. This is the heart of my revelation.

There is a huge round of applause and many shouts of 'Alleluia!'

MIKE: I know we're pushed for time, but could you describe at least some parts of your visions?

JOHN: When you get to read the book, you'll discover the *lamb*, which symbolizes Jesus, who gave up his life as a sacrifice for us all.

You'll come across the *four horse riders* who represent conquest, war, famine and death.

I saw visions of a *dragon* with seven heads and ten horns. This was Satan. Then there was the *prostitute of Babylon*. This character symbolized the city of Rome. Whether it's now, or many years in the future, every age will always have its 'Babylon', a power fighting against Christianity. These are just a few of the many characters I saw.

The final visions I received were beautiful. I saw a new heaven and earth. I saw God's work being completed through the work of Jesus. This new world was totally unspoiled by human sin. It filled my heart and soul with hope and joy, as I hope it will for all of you. It's wonderful when I think how, in Genesis, the whole story started with the beautiful garden of Eden, and my final vision is that of the city of God.

The audience go wild with applause and shouts of 'Alleluia!'

MIKE: Wow! I actually had a tear or two in my eyes, listening to that powerful description of your final vision. Those are real words of hope.

Before the show, John, you were telling me that your revelations are also about the end of time. Do you know when this will be and how it will happen?

JOHN: The revelation I received was about how God will judge Rome and how that empire will fall, but the revelations were also about how God will defeat evil once and for all. What I saw gave me great encouragement. God will defeat the evil of Rome and, in time, will defeat all evil. But there was nothing in my revelations that stated when this final triumph over evil would happen.

MIKE: When we finally get to read your words, your 'revelation', should we be looking for hidden meanings? Will some folk be able to work out when the end of time may come?

JOHN: A good question, Mike, and this was one reason why I wondered if I should tell anybody about these visions. I don't want people making up their own ideas about what it means. My visions are not strange codes that somebody else needs to work out. I would warn anybody against ever doing this. The words I will write down will be words of great poetry, aiming to encourage people and give them hope that God will one day finally defeat the powers of evil and darkness. That is all I want people to understand from this revelation. Enjoy reading it; and may you find comfort in it. Do not be foolish and try to see things in the words that simply aren't there. God bless you all.

The audience applaud John, and look very excited about his revelation.

MIKE: Once again, this show is far too short! John, you've been a wonderful guest. Thanks for everything you've shared with us this evening and a big thank you for choosing us to be the first to hear about the visions you had on Patmos. We'll help you get to Ephesus now, and we look forward to reading your book of Revelation in full. Ladies and gentlemen, a huge round of applause for John.

The audience stand and clap enthusiastically. Many people shout out, 'God bless you, John! Good luck.'

Sadly, next week is the final show in this series.

The audience all boo. Many shout out 'Shame!' They are clearly disappointed that there is only one show left.

You're too kind! Next week's show promises to be just as exciting. Our last guest in the series is Paul, and already most places in the audience have been booked by women! I hope Paul knows what he's letting himself in for. We've managed to get a day-release from prison for him, and we're very lucky to have him on the show. So, until then, thank you for being here tonight. God bless.

Audience applaud.

---

41 This is the Greek for 'sons of thunder' or 'men of thunder'.

42 Gnosticism was a widespread religious movement, which surfaced in the Roman Empire. The term Gnosticism comes from the Greek word *gnosis*, which means 'knowledge', especially revealed religious knowledge necessary for salvation. Gnostics believed that the world was an evil place, and the only way to be liberated from it was secretly revealed knowledge about God, the world, and the origin, condition and destiny of humankind.

43 This phrase was actually used by Winston Churchill in 1939 when he described Russia.

44 Greek-speaking Jews influenced by Greek philosophy.

45 John 8:12.

46 From the Greek meaning 'the word'.

47 John 1:1–5.

48 John 1:14.

49 Exodus 3:14.

50 John 6:35.

51 John 8:12; 9:5.

52 John 10:7, 9.

53 John 10:11.

54 John 11:25.

55 John 4:6.

56 John 15:1, 5.

57 John 14:5.

58 John 14:6.

59 It would have been about 600 to 700 litres of wine!

60 John 2:11.

61 Isaiah 9:1–2.

62 An example of this can be seen in Mark 7:3–4.

63 John 2:10.

64 John 11:1–44.

65 John 11:4.

66 John 11:43.

67 John 11:25.

68 1 John 1:5.

69 Mark 5:35–43.

70 Mark 9:2–9.

71 Mark 14:32–42.

Mike Coles chats to Paul

MIKE: Ladies and gentlemen, welcome to the last show in this series. I've been looking forward to this one for ages now, and I know you're all dying to meet our guest as well. I'm sorry we had no musical introduction today. This is because we need every second we have for today's guest! We have a packed house here, and I notice how many women there are, all sitting at the front. I know you'll be giving my guest a wonderful, warm welcome!

Many of the audience laugh at this.

Like all of my guests so far, we probably need about a year to have a really decent conversation. At one stage, my guest was a Pharisee who viciously persecuted the first Christians, and gave the word on occasions to have some of them killed. On one of his missions to seek out and arrest Christians, he had an awesome encounter with the risen Jesus. He became a believer, and for thirty years he has travelled the Roman Empire preaching the good news. He has founded many churches; he has been picked on and persecuted, thrown into prison. When he's had time, he's written letters to churches giving advice and encouragement, and this is just a tiny part of what this man has done. I know that in some of his letters he's had certain things to say about the role of women in worship and their role in life generally. I guess this is why we have so many women here today, eager to meet my guest and, no doubt, ask him many questions!

Without wasting any more time, as these shows never last long, please welcome that great apostle, Paul!

As well as a deafening cheer and round of applause for Paul from most of the audience, many of the women start booing and jeering.

MIKE: Wow! What a welcome!

'Do you want us to sit here in silence, Paul, or are we allowed to speak later in the show?' shouts one of the women at the front. Many of the audience laugh.

I do apologize, Paul, but to be honest, I was expecting this.

PAUL: Thank you all for your welcome, and may God's peace be with you. If I could quickly say before the next outburst from anyone in the audience, I will be happy to discuss anything and explain any of my teachings if you could just give me a chance to speak. I hope you may be pleasantly surprised at what I have to say.

'We'd better be pleasantly surprised. Your teachings haven't impressed us women much so far!'

MIKE: Well, as Paul has said, he's willing to talk about any of his teachings and views throughout the show, so let's give him a chance.

I've really been looking forward to this show, Paul; you're very welcome. I'm glad you could get a day-release from house arrest in Rome to be with us. Before we get on to more specific aspects of your teaching, I think it's vital that we hear a little about your life up to and including that moment when you met the risen Lord Jesus on your journey from Jerusalem to Damascus.

PAUL: Well, many of you know that I was born into a very strict Jewish family in Tarsus.[72] I wasn't always called Paul. I was originally named Saul, after the ancient Hebrew king. I was circumcised on the eighth day as stipulated by the Jewish Law, and I was brought up in accordance with the Pharisaic interpretation of the Law.

MIKE: Why the name change to Paul?

PAUL: Quite simply, I just decided to use the Latin name Paul, which of course is very similar to my Hebrew birth name.

MIKE: Tell us about your general education.

PAUL: As a young lad in Tarsus, I learned a great deal about Greek rhetoric, as you've probably guessed from reading some of my letters. Perhaps the most important thing you need to understand, before I discuss my experience on the road to Damascus, is that the main influence on my life at that stage was the formal training in the Jewish Law that I received in preparation for becoming a rabbi. It was no ordinary education, either. I was lucky to have as my teacher that well-known man, Gamaliel the Elder. In some of my letters, I've written about how I was a perfect student. In my letter to the Philippians I wrote, 'As far as a person can be righteous by obeying the commands of the Law, I was faultless.'[73]

MIKE: Did this faultless obedience to the Law make you happy? Were you spiritually fulfilled?

PAUL: Far from it, Mike. Every waking hour of my life was spent reading and learning, and painfully trying to follow every letter of the Law. But I was never happy. Despite all this knowledge of the Law and all my great learning, I was empty inside, although I hoped that with more and more study, things might eventually change.

With this zeal I had for studying the Law, I was led to persecuting the ever-growing Christian Church. I thought I might get some fulfil-ment out of doing this. I saw these Christians as being some sort of heretical Jewish sect: they were untrue to the Law and should therefore be wiped out.

But this didn't help me either. I began to despair of ever achieving any sort of peace and happiness. One of the biggest turning points in my life, just before I met the risen Lord, was when I witnessed the stoning of Stephen, the first martyr for our faith. The members of the Council and myself were all surrounding him. We were furious, but he stood there with a radiant and happy face. He was full of the Holy Spirit, looking up into heaven. He spoke those words that I'll never forget: 'Look! I can see heaven opened and the Son of Man standing at the right-hand side of God!'[74] It was at this point that he was taken out and stoned to death. Just before he died, he even managed to ask God to forgive us for stoning him.

This whole incident made me so angry. Not because he was a Christian, or because of what he was saying. I was furious because he was so happy and content. I had never experienced for a second what this man Stephen had. What gave him the strength and encouragement, even in the face of death, to be so happy and to pray that we'd be forgiven for stoning him? He seemed so free. Why couldn't I experience this freedom? I knew the Law better than anyone. If anybody should be happy and free, it should have been me! Instead of trying to find answers to these questions of mine, I just became more violent, and increased my threats of murder to anyone who followed this Lord Jesus.

MIKE: Of course, it was at this moment in your life that God helped you to understand what could truly free you. You met the risen Lord Jesus.

PAUL: God knew exactly when to step into my life. I couldn't have gone on much longer the way I was—terribly unhappy, full of anger and, indeed, jealousy of these Christians who seemed to have what I had been striving for all my life.

As I mentioned earlier, I was travelling to Damascus, hunting for more Christians to arrest and put to death. On the way I had an awesome and shocking encounter with the risen Lord. I was surrounded by bright light from the sky and I heard a voice saying, 'Saul, Saul! Why are you persecuting me?'[75] Eventually I found out that it was Jesus who was speaking to me. He told me to go into the city and wait for instructions. After the brightness of the light, I was blinded for three days. A Christian called Ananias came and placed his hands on me so that I was able to see again.

MIKE: It must have been pretty brave of Ananias to come and see you, knowing that you were coming to have people like him put to death!

Audience laugh.

PAUL: That's one of the first things Ananias and I spoke about. I told him that only a fool would have come and spoken to me, had they been a Christian. We both laughed about it. He told me how God had led him to me. It was then that I was baptized and filled with the Holy Spirit. The only phrase I can use to explain how I felt is 'born again'. A whole lifetime of studying the Law had never led me to feel the way I did at this moment. I was free. I was full of the Holy Spirit. I was happy, amazingly happy.

I had met Jesus alive, risen from the dead, and he had called me to be an apostle, an apostle to the Gentiles.

MIKE: I have to say, Paul, that an apostle to the Gentiles you have most certainly been, and quite remarkably.

The audience applaud and praise Paul. Even the women in the front applaud, but it's quite clear from their general lack of enthusiasm that they have something else on their minds, many of them eager for a chance to ask questions.

After your conversion, Paul…

PAUL: Sorry to interrupt you there, Mike. It's just that quite a few people use the term 'conversion' to describe my experience on the road to Damascus. I have never used this term myself to describe that unique experience. It sounds as if I converted from one religion to another. That wasn't the case. Jesus revealed himself to me to show that everything, all religions, are fulfilled in him.

MIKE: Isn't that what you wrote in your letter to the Galatians? 'There is no difference between Jews and Gentiles… you are all one in union with Christ Jesus.'[76]

'Hey! What about the rest of that verse, Mike, the bit about no difference between men and women?' shouts one of the women in the audience.

Yes, I realize what a crucial verse that is to you, and, as I promised at the beginning, we will be able to discuss all of this with Paul. You were saying, Paul…

PAUL: Rather than 'conversion', I simply like to say that God 'called' me. I was called to be a Christian, and my call was to be an evangelist to the Gentiles. I understood Peter's necessary mission to the Jews, but God called me to let the whole world know that Christ is for everybody, not just the Jews. Sorry to have interrupted you earlier, Mike. What were you were going to ask me?

MIKE: Only a few days after your 'calling', you went straight to the synagogues in Damascus and started preaching that Jesus was the Son of God. How did you know what to say?

PAUL: In some of my letters, Mike, I answer your question quite clearly. In my letter to the Galatians I clearly told them that the gospel I was preaching was not of human origin. I didn't receive it from any human being. It was Jesus Christ himself who revealed it to me.[77]

MIKE: I know that in Damascus your message was so powerful that the Jews had no idea what to say against your claim that Jesus was the Messiah. They eventually got so annoyed with you that they wanted you dead. I bet you could understand this!

PAUL: Yes, I knew exactly how they felt! It was only a week or so before this that I had been furious with the Christians and wanting them dead. But things got so bad that I had to escape from the city. Some of my followers let me down in a basket through an opening in the city wall.

MIKE: And so your story began. What an adventure! We know about your three amazing missionary journeys. What was the driving force behind these journeys?

PAUL: When reading my letters, you'll notice that I had three aims. First, I wanted to go and spread the wonderful news about Jesus to places not yet visited by other Christian missionaries. In my letter to the Romans, I wrote about my plan to travel as far west as Spain.[78] I also wrote in Romans that I have an obligation to people everywhere, to the civilized and uncivilized, to those educated and ignorant.[79]

Second, having founded many churches, it was my responsibility to help these new congregations to grow. I would revisit many of them and help them when they had problems. I had to visit Corinth many times!

Finally, the other task I had was to collect money from the many Gentile churches I had set up and deliver this collection to the Jewish Christian church in Jerusalem, to help the church grow and support those who needed it. By doing this, I hoped to bring the Gentile churches together with those of the Jewish Christians.

MIKE: You finally ended up in Rome, after being arrested in Jerusalem, thanks to the riots incited by your many Jewish opponents. How is life for you in Rome at the moment?

PAUL: Things are fine, thank you, Mike. As you know, I'm living under house arrest in rented accommodation. I'm treated well, have many visitors, and I'm still able to carry out the Lord's work. I've been there nearly two years now, and I'm hoping to stand trial pretty soon. I have a good feeling that the trial will go well and that I'll be released. I still hope to visit Spain.

MIKE: We wish you well with your trial, Paul.

The audience applaud in support of these good wishes.

If you don't mind now, Paul, I would like to take some questions from the audience. There's a fair bit of unrest and fidgeting in the front few rows, and I'd like some of the women to ask their questions. By the way, I would appreciate it if the lady in the third row would remove her placard. It's not very respectful and certainly isn't very Christian.

Most of the audience agree with Mike, saying 'Hear! Hear!' as she removes her placard, which states that 'PAUL IS A SEXIST PIG!'

PAUL: I'm sorry the lady feels like that. I would hope that, after I've answered some of your questions, you'll come to realize that I am far from being a 'sexist pig'.

MIKE: We'll get straight down to our first question, then. In fact, would the lady in the third row who was holding the placard like to ask Paul the first question? I'm sure there's plenty you'd like to ask, seeing as you think he's nothing but a sexist pig! Why do you think this? What's your question?

'Thanks. I'd love to ask Paul a couple of questions, if that's OK. My name's Sarah and I'm from Corinth.'

PAUL: Hello, Sarah, my dear sister in Christ.

'Please don't "dear sister" me, Paul. If that's how you see me and other women—as dear sisters—why on earth, in your first letter to my church in Corinth, did you write, "In all the churches of God's people, the women

should keep quiet in the meetings. They are not allowed to speak, just as the Jewish Law says, they are not allowed to be in charge. If they ever want to find out about something, they should ask their husbands at home. It's a disgraceful thing for a woman to speak in church"?[80]

'All around us, women are treated like dirt. I recently heard a Jewish rabbi say that each day a man must pronounce three blessings: "Blessed be the Lord who did not make me a heathen; blessed be he who did not make me a woman; and blessed be he who did not make me an uneducated person."[81]

'This is just one example of many showing how badly we women are treated today. But through Christ this should have all changed. Even you, Paul, wrote in your letter to the Galatians, "There is neither Jew nor Greek, slave nor free, male nor female, for you are all one in Christ Jesus."[82] How on earth can you then write what you did to my church, that it is disgraceful for a woman to speak in church?'

Sarah gets a huge round of applause from the front part of the audience.

MIKE: Straight over to you, Paul!

Audience laugh.

PAUL: Thanks, Mike, and thank you, Sarah, for your question. I am well aware of the horrendous attitude that there is towards woman today. I have to be honest and tell you that, when training to be a rabbi a good few years ago, many of us were encouraged not to teach or even speak with women. I was taught the saying, 'From garments cometh a moth and from a woman the iniquities of a man.'[83]

Many of the audience gasp at this, obviously disgusted.

MIKE: I remember chatting to Luke a couple of weeks ago. He also mentioned how badly women are treated.

PAUL: Perhaps all those years ago I *was* a bit of a 'sexist pig', and as you also know, I was not a happy man, never fulfilled. But through meeting the risen Lord, and discovering a whole new relationship with God, I have learned to enjoy a new freedom in my relationships with other people. As Sarah pointed out, I write to the Galatians that it simply makes no difference whether these people are men or women, Jews or Gentiles, slaves or masters, educated or ignorant. I have come to see that we are all of equal value to God.

The audience applaud. One woman then shouts out, 'That's great, Paul, but what about this keeping our mouths shut in church—the idea that it's a disgrace for us to talk in church?'

MIKE: I'm sure that if you give Paul half a chance he will answer this question. Perhaps it's all this shouting and heckling you're doing that Paul is talking about when he says that women must remain quiet!

Many of the audience laugh and applaud at this! But some of the women 'boo' at Mike's comment, not impressed with his sense of humour.

PAUL: Of course women can speak in church. You've totally misunderstood what I've been teaching! In my first letter to the Corinthians I wrote, 'And any woman who prays or proclaims God's message in public worship...'[84] We are all equal in Christ, and women can certainly preach God's message in church. When I wrote about women not being able to speak in church, I was simply referring to some women chattering and gossiping away when a service was in progress. We can't have meetings being disturbed like that! Women can take part in formal lectures, exhortation and teaching. It's the general chatter that I was warning against; and of course I would give exactly the same warning to the men if I ever received any complaints about similar behaviour from them.

Some of the women give Paul a little round of applause at this point. Is he slowly winning them over?

MIKE: Paul, if I could just take you back a little. You mentioned your letter to the Corinthians, where you wrote about 'any woman who prays or proclaims God's message in public worship...', but you didn't complete the whole verse, as it continues '... with nothing on her head disgraces her husband'. Could you explain that to us, please?

PAUL: My only concern in that part of my letter[85] is to make the point that women need to maintain their sexual identity as women, and this needs to be reflected in what they're wearing. Any woman who is appointed to a leadership position in the church isn't adopting a male role; but neither, of course, is she going to stand in front of the congregation as a sex object. With her head uncovered and hair flowing, some men in the congregation might look at her as a beautiful woman and pay no attention to what she has to say. She needs to make sure that her hair and shoulders are covered because she stands before God as man's equal, not just as some sex object, an object of man's desire. So, when you look at it like this, the veil she wears is a symbol of her authority. This authority is given to her by God as a result of the work of Jesus in whom 'there is neither male nor female'.[86]

The audience applaud these clarifications enthusiastically. Many of the women in the front are warming to Paul a little now. His last few words certainly seem to have impressed many of them.

MIKE: Well, Paul, some great words there. I really was wondering what you'd be saying today to the many women present. Just before the show I was afraid we might have a riot on our hands, but the way you're explaining many of your teachings makes perfect sense. Nothing sexist about you at the moment! Let's go for another question. How about the lady right here in the front, in the blue and green. What's your name and what's your question for Paul?

'Hello. My name's Leah. I agree with Mike. I am quite surprised at what I'm hearing. I came here looking for a real scrap with Paul today, because

of what I thought was his disgraceful teaching about women. But I'll let him carry on explaining himself before I make my mind up about him. I also need to make it clear that many of us women here do admire Paul in many ways. He's worked miracles in spreading the gospel, and bringing the message to the Gentiles, and it's been no easy task for him. Our concern, of course, is the way he has seemed to treat and regard women. We've come along today to find out what these teachings of his are actually all about, because on the surface they do sound so sexist!

'The passage that I would like Paul to explain is what he wrote to the Ephesians: "Men and women should submit to one another out of reverence for Christ. Wives, submit to your husbands as to the Lord. For the husband is the head of the wife as Christ is the head of the church." [87] *Must I submit to my husband?'*

MIKE: I was waiting for someone to bring this up! All yours, Paul. How are you going to explain this one? By the way, thanks for the question, Leah.

PAUL: I'd like to say the following about that passage: just focus on the very first part, where I write, 'Submit to one another out of reverence for Christ.' That's the key point. There needs to be mutual submission, and interdependence. The head and the body are interdependent, after all! To all those who are married I simply say, 'Submit to one another out of reverence for Christ.'

Paul seems to have done the trick. The audience go wild at this. Many of the women stand up in the front and cheer.

MIKE: I think I've just witnessed a miracle!

Audience laugh.

I have to say, that was pretty amazing stuff, Paul. Thank you so much for straightening things out there.

I'd like to leave this issue now, especially as Paul has ended on such a positive note. It seems to me that many of the women here today are much happier about some of his teachings, having heard him explain himself.

Usually we would have an advert or a bit of music at this part of the show, but the time zooms by so fast, and we still have so much that we want to chat to Paul about that we'll just carry straight on. I've received a few letters and I'd like to read one or two out, if that's OK.

I've had a letter from a chap called Luke, but he doesn't tell us where he's from.

PAUL: It's not my beloved doctor, is it?

The audience laugh at this.

MIKE: No, no, Paul! It's definitely not from him, although if we have time, which is unlikely, we could chat about him a bit later. It's quite a long letter, so I'll just sum it up. Luke has recently become a Christian.

'Praise the Lord!' shout some of the audience.

However, there are some people in his church who keep telling him that before he can become a true Christian, he has to become a Jew. Luke is very confused and would like to know what he must do.

'He must become a Jew first!' calls out a man from the back of the audience.

'Rubbish!' shouts someone else. 'It's faith in Jesus alone that puts us right with God!'

The first man yells back, 'Gentiles must be circumcised first and made to obey the Law. Then comes the faith in Jesus!'

PAUL (standing up): Silence! Please listen to what I have to say now. I'm getting quite annoyed with this whole issue. This is my answer to Luke's question and this is what I have to say to you all in the audience today, especially to my brother in Christ there at the back who believes that Gentiles must first become Jews before becoming Christians.

Earlier on, I explained how unhappy I was, trying to please God by keeping the Old Testament Law. It's impossible, believe me! It was because of this impossibility that Jesus came. He showed us a new way to love and please God. If we try to cling on to these old laws, then what was the point of Jesus coming in the first place?

By listening to the gospel, we have received that wonderful gift of the Holy Spirit. It is by the power of the Spirit that we know how to live our lives. Are the Judaizers[88] saying that we should exchange this power for our own weak willpower and follow the Law? Absolute nonsense!

Most of the audience applaud and cheer at this.

I wrote to the Galatians, 'Freedom is what we all have. Christ has set us free! Stand, then, as free people, and don't allow yourselves to become slaves again.'[89] When I followed the Law to the letter, I was a slave to sin and guilt. That's what following the Law does. Let us value this wonderful freedom we have through Christ.

At this point, the man at the back gets up and storms out, obviously disgusted at what Paul has said.

I pray that our brother will soon come to know this freedom that we can enjoy. Let us all remember him in our prayers.

The final point I need to make is that this freedom Christ has given us should be used to do good. It's not an excuse for us to start behaving badly, or to let our 'physical desires control us'.[90] As I always say, the whole Law can be summed up as follows: 'Love your neighbour as you love yourself.'[91]

MIKE: You also mention in your letter to the Galatians that the Spirit produces love, peace, joy, patience, kindness, goodness, faithfulness, humility and self-control.[92] Surely, following the Law letter by letter cannot do this; only the Holy Spirit can.

I hope that has helped, Luke, and any others out there who have been experiencing the same problem.

Going back to the many letters I have received, quite a few of them want to know what it's like, travelling around as you have done. Some of the people who have written in have never left their home village, town or city. To them, you seem to have travelled the whole world. What's it been like?

PAUL: What a question! Well, I have to say from the beginning, whatever we might think of the Romans, and whatever they might think of us (which is not a lot), I'd like to thank them for making it so easy for me to spread the gospel!

MIKE: Don't let them know that, Paul! How on earth have they helped you?

PAUL: Well, for a start, there is peace right across their empire. The frontiers are easy to cross, there are no pirates on the seas, and of course we all know about their roads. They're straight, really quick, and you can take a Roman road to pretty much anywhere! All these factors made it much easier for me in my travels. God has obviously used the Romans to help in preaching the gospel! Thank you, Lord, for the Romans!

The audience really love this point and laugh and cheer.

As far as the actual travelling goes, I would normally ride a mule or walk, depending on how I was feeling. I used to meet all sorts of people on the roads. There'd often be chariots charging by with soldiers, or carrying the imperial post. I used to see many passenger coaches and carriages transporting the wealthy folk around. Whenever I got the chance, I would try to chat to those I met on the way, and tell them about Christ, often winning them over to the Lord.

MIKE: I hope you don't mind me interrupting here, Paul, but you just mentioned that you would either walk or ride on your mule, depending on *how you were feeling*. This is something many of us are dying to know. Is there a medical problem that has been troubling you for years? When I chatted to Luke in a previous show, he very professionally maintained confidentiality and wouldn't say what your problem was. You also wrote in your second letter to the Corinthians that God gave you a 'thorn in the flesh', to beat you and to save you from becoming proud.[93] If you don't mind, could you tell us what this 'thorn in the flesh' is?

PAUL: Ever since I wrote that letter and mentioned the 'thorn in the flesh', so many people have been asking me what was wrong with me. Also, because I travelled around a fair bit with Luke, my 'beloved doctor', everyone thinks I had some kind of awful illness. How do I look to you, Mike?

MIKE: Well, to be honest, Paul, I've never seen anyone looking so well!

PAUL: There you go! I can't even remember the last time I felt ill—except that I did eat some dodgy fish a few weeks ago, but I won't go into too much detail about that!

Some of the audience giggle.

Let me explain what I meant when I wrote about the 'thorn in my flesh'. In no way was I referring to any physical ailment. If I had any sickness like that, you'd notice it today, and how could I have done all that travelling if I had been so ill? If I'd had this awful physical ailment, sick people would have just laughed at me when I went around preaching about God's healing power!

Audience laugh.

When I talk about this thorn in my side, I am referring to a demonic spirit sent by Satan to annoy me. When I was attacked or persecuted, or laughed at, this was all the work of Satan, the continual thorn in my side.[94] Some days it was awful, and I'd feel very low. Luke always helped me snap out of it. It wasn't that I was ever ill, it was Satan continually obstructing me, tormenting and annoying me.

The saying 'thorn in my side' has been used often before and has never meant an illness. In the book of Judges, the Lord said to the children of Israel, 'I tell you all now, I will not drive these people out as you advance. They will be like thorns in your sides.'[95]

Anyway, I hope that makes it clearer for you. I seem to have been confusing you on many issues—my health, women…

The audience laugh.

MIKE: If there has been a little confusion on some issues, there certainly isn't now. It's fantastic that you're here today, and we're really enjoying listening to you.

The audience applaud here, totally agreeing with Mike. The women at the front seem like different people, compared to how they were at the start of the show! They are all smiling and nodding in agreement with what Mike is saying.

I interrupted you earlier, Paul; you were telling us about your travelling.

PAUL: That's right. I was telling you how helpful the Romans have been in helping me travel with their marvellous roads. Travelling wasn't always easy, though. I'm not usually one for moaning, but in my second letter to the Corinthians I explained how, during my many travels, I have been threatened by floods and robbers. There were times when I went hungry, didn't have decent shelter or clothes.[96] I had some exciting times at sea as well. I would normally travel at sea between May and September, the safe sailing season, but

I'm sure you've all heard about my voyage to Rome in the month of October. The storm was like nothing you've ever seen before; we were shipwrecked, and ended up in Malta. That was a real adventure! Luke has written an account of the whole journey.[97] Maybe another time I could tell you about it in more detail.

MIKE: Well, we can't let you get away without hearing a bit about your shipwreck. Tell us about what happened on Malta; if I remember correctly, didn't a snake attack you?

PAUL: There were 276 of us shipwrecked—sailors, prisoners, passengers and soldiers—but we all survived. The Lord was certainly watching over us.

MIKE: Throughout the storm and shipwreck you remained totally calm. You seemed to know all along that you would be saved.

PAUL: I always knew that it wasn't the Jews or Romans who were sending me to Rome: it was God. Christ had instructed me to bear witness also at Rome.[98] I knew I would reach the city, but I didn't expect the journey to be so difficult. Like any man, I was terrified at times. The waves were like mountains! But I held on to Christ's words that I had to go to Rome. The storm and shipwreck were that 'thorn in my side' again—Satan doing his best to prevent me spreading the gospel. But he'll need to do better than that if he's going to stop me!

Audience laugh.

Mike, you asked about a snake attacking me. What happened is that we all got safely ashore[99] and met the people living on the island. They were very friendly and made us welcome. As it was drizzling, they made us a fire. I went to collect some wood, but as I put some on the fire, a snake wriggled out and immediately bit my hand. The locals saw this and thought that, as I was a prisoner, I must be some sort of murderer and this was now my punishment. They waited for me to swell up or drop down dead! But I remember Luke telling me never to panic if bitten by a snake, as this can make the poison spread quickly. So I didn't panic. I just shook the snake off into the fire.

What happened next did make me laugh. When the people saw that I was fine, they decided I must be a 'god'! One minute a murderer, now a god!

The audience laugh, obviously relishing hearing Paul's adventures at first hand.

MIKE: A wonderful story! We know that you healed the sick people on that island as well. I wish we had time to listen to some of the many other adventures you have had. But sadly, time is getting on and I'm conscious that not many of the audience have had a chance to ask a question. The few that have been asked were mainly from women about women. So we'll go straight over to the audience again for a few more questions.

The chap sitting in the second row from the back. No, not you, sir, the man next to you. Yes, you, with the curly hair.

'My name's Andrew. I wanted to know whether I could have a quick word with Paul after the show as I'm in the tent-making business, and I'd like a few business tips.'

PAUL: May I say what a fine line of work you're in, Andrew. I'd be delighted to have a quick chat with you after the show. I haven't made a tent in quite a while. It'll be nice to catch up with the news in the trade!

MIKE: A nice short question with a short answer. Let's move straight on. How about the gentleman sitting opposite me, four rows from the front. Yes, you, sir.

'Hi. My name is Barnabas. I hope you don't mind me asking, Paul, but why are you still single? I always thought it was God's intention from the very beginning with Adam and Eve that we should all marry. You must miss having a woman by your side. What about the physical side? How do you cope? Not meaning to sound rude or offensive, but I often used to think that maybe the continual thorn in your side was because you were single, and had strong urges from time to time!'

The audience are quite shocked at this, and eagerly await Paul's reply.

PAUL: I'm not offended, Barnabas. The fact that I'm a single chap is because this is what God wants for me. I have chosen celibacy; it's actually a gift God has given me. I say 'gift', because I don't burn with desire all day, lusting after women. It's something I don't have to worry about, so my whole life and energy are used to spread the good news. We all believe that Christ will soon return, so I believe it's better to use the time we have left wisely, and prepare for the kingdom. I'd like it if you could all be celibate like me.

Many of the audience laugh here. 'It's not for me, thanks, Paul!' shouts a man from the back.

'I have a gorgeous wife and I love her to bits! No celibacy for me, thank you very much!' shouts someone else.

I realize that this is something God wanted for me. We all receive different gifts. I know I would like you all to be celibate as well, but only if you truly feel this is what God wants for you. I know about these strong sexual urges, and of course you mustn't fight against them. By all means marry. It's far better to do so than spend all your time thinking about sex and then perhaps being led into sin.

Barnabas interrupts: 'I'm sorry, Paul, but I'm really going to have to disagree with you. I respect your choice to remain celibate, but I think you rather look down on those of us who are married. In your first letter to the

Corinthians you wrote to them, "To the unmarried and the widows I say that it is better for them to remain single like me. But if they can't control themselves, then they should marry. It would be better for them to marry than to burn with passion." [100] *This makes us married folk sound a little unworthy as far as you're concerned. We were obviously sex-mad and couldn't control ourselves so we had to get married. But God made us like this! It's natural to have sexual feelings, fall in love and marry. If you don't mind me saying, Paul, I think it's you who have got things wrong. You don't know what you're missing out on.'*

The audience applaud very loudly.

MIKE: Poor old Paul! You've really had to defend yourself here today. Not to make things any worse, I do have to agree with what Barnabas said. To you, Paul, just the mention of sex means 'sin', and I think the only reason you support marriage at all is that it's the best way to contain this awful, sinful thing—sex!

PAUL: Once again, I think I have been totally misunderstood. I would like to apologize to Barnabas and anyone else who is married who feels that I have referred to them as inferior to me because I have been blessed with the gift of celibacy.

'You call that a gift?' shouts a member of the audience.

MIKE: With the show slowly coming to an end, please let's give Paul a chance to explain himself. It takes a brave man to sit here and explain his views on sex and marriage in front of you lot!

PAUL: Thank you, Mike. I am aware that I do sometimes ramble on and maybe say things in a rather over-the-top way. But you need to understand where I'm coming from. When I wrote to the Corinthians, I was disgusted with what I heard was going on in their city— sleeping with prostitutes, orgies, sexual immorality everywhere. This is why I have such strong views. Whenever I am dealing with sexual matters, it always involves the most awful and disgusting sinful behaviour. That's why my immediate response is 'Why can't you be celibate like me, and not get involved with all this filth?'

Barnabas, I'm glad you respect my point of view. I do believe that celibacy is the best way in this day and age, but that's my personal view. I don't want folk ever to think that I consider myself better in any way compared to those who marry.

MIKE: So, Paul, in a nutshell, what's your view on sex?

PAUL: In its right place, sex is a wonderful gift from God. I remind you all that your bodies are temples of the Holy Spirit. Your bodies are parts of the body of Christ. If you marry, and enjoy sexual relations within marriage, that is something holy and God-given, and the body remains pure and holy. From the very beginning it was meant to be that a man leaves his father and mother and is united with his wife, and they become one.[101] I'll leave it at that now, in case I start to go on again and offend someone. I hope that's explained things a little.

The audience applaud.

MIKE: Once again, a pretty good response, Paul. However, I do know that many folk here today would still love to ask you plenty more questions on this whole issue of sex and marriage. Many of the letters I have received also refer to this whole area. I think we'll have to give you your own show. We can call it 'To touch, or not to touch? That is the question'.

Just before the end of what has been a great show, I think we have time for one more question from the audience. The lady in the front row with the deep purple robe. Yes, you, madam. What's your question for Paul?

'Thank you very much for letting me ask the last question. My name is Tamar. I'm afraid my question is going to be another tough one for Paul.

122

It's nothing personal, and I must say I have been very impressed with many of his comments and teachings this evening.

'Paul, you continually talk about the body of Christ, one Church and so on, but when I look around and hear reports of what's going on, the only church I'm aware of is a badly divided church.

'I'm sorry to mention Corinth, as they've already had a bad press about the sexual immorality going on there, but they have all sorts of factions in their so-called church. There are those people who profess their adherence to you, Paul, others to Apollos, others to Peter and some to Christ. There are also factions between the rich and poor.

'As we heard earlier in the show, some believe that Gentiles need to adhere to Judaism through the act of circumcision, and of course others like you, Paul, maintain that they are totally misunderstanding the real message of the gospel.

'What on earth is going on? Where is this one Body of Christ?'

MIKE: A nice easy one for you to finish on, Paul!

Audience laugh.

PAUL: The picture you paint of the church is not a pretty one, Tamar, and in many respects you are right. There are no magic answers. You know that in all my letters I continually stress the great importance of unity, and I also openly rebuke those who I believe are responsible for the many divisions present in the church.

What more can I say but to emphasize that we are all parts of the one body, and all these parts have different functions. Despite all these parts, despite how many of us there are, we are all one in union with Christ.[102]

This has been repeated many times throughout the show, but I'll say it again: you were all baptized into union with Christ. You are all, so to speak, clothed in Christ. For this reason there is neither Jew nor Greek, neither slave nor free, male or female. You are all one in Christ Jesus.[103]

Only one thing can produce this unity, my dear brothers and sisters, and that is *love*. Only love will create perfect harmony in our church. As I wrote to the church in Colossae, 'Above all these things, I urge you to put on love, which binds everything together in perfect harmony.'[104]

The audience applaud Paul here. Many shout out, 'Amen!'

Before Paul can continue, Tamar immediately interrupts, saying, 'That's all well and good, you preaching about love, but if I'm honest I sometimes feel you show the opposite in your attitude to some people.'

Many of the audience are quite shocked at this. The atmosphere suddenly becomes a little tenser, as it was when the issue of women was first raised at the start of the show. The audience goes silent again, and Tamar continues.

'When you wrote to the Galatians, you said that if anyone preaches a gospel to them which is different to the one they received, they are to be condemned to hell! And there are other examples like this. These terrible judgments that you make on people who disagree with you cause more divisions than anything else in the church! Where's the love now, Paul?'

Some members of the audience start to boo at Tamar.

'If anyone is causing divisions, it's you! Be quiet!' shouts a man from the back of the audience.

MIKE: Now, now. It's almost time to finish, and it would be a terrible shame to end on a bad note. I'd like Paul to have the final word in response to Tamar's concerns.

PAUL: Dear Tamar, all I ever want is to preach and teach the message of Christ's love to you all. It's as simple as that. The words I speak are from Christ himself. I simply speak the truth. And those of you who live and walk in the truth will know Christ's love.

When I speak sternly to people, it's because they say things that destroy Christ's message. When people do this, they bring confusion into the community and sow seeds of doubt. It's an evil among us. Satan is behind it all. It's because of the love I have for you all that I do speak most harshly to anyone who might destroy our holy community. My dear sister Tamar, it's those who wish to cause divisions among us that you must be aware of, not me. As I said to the Ephesians, I now fall upon my knees before God the Father, from whom every family in heaven and on earth receives its true name. I ask God in all his glory to give you the power through his Spirit to be strong in your inner selves. I pray that Christ will make his home in your hearts through faith. I pray that you may have your roots and foundation in love, so that you, together with all God's people, may have the power to understand how long and broad, high and deep, Christ's love is. I pray that you may all come to know his love, although it will never be fully known, and that you may all be filled with the very nature of God.[105]

At this the audience go wild. Paul gets a standing ovation. There are huge cheers. People shout out, 'God bless you, Paul!'

MIKE: Amazing, Paul. No matter what the question or criticism, your wisdom brings peace to every situation. You have been honest with us here today. Your work has been nothing short of a miracle. It has been an honour talking to you. Many people came here con-fused, some were angry and some were concerned about the many divisions in the church, but listening to your words has been a real blessing.

I could chat to you for ever, Paul. There is so much more we could have talked about. All I can say is thank you so much for being with us, and sharing Christ's message and your amazing story. It's a wonderful ending to the series *So you think you're a New Testament writer*. Perhaps we'll get a chance to speak to you again in another show. God bless you, Paul.

PAUL: May the grace of the Lord Jesus Christ be with you all.

There is a massive round of applause, which seems to go on for ages.

72 Now in Turkey.

73 Philippians 3:6.

74 Acts 7:56.

75 Acts 9:4.

76 Galatians 3:28.

77 Galatians 1:11–12.

78 Romans 15:24.

79 Romans 1:14.

80 1 Corinthians 14:34–35.

81 Rabbi Judah, a contemporary of the first-century Jewish historian Flavius Josephus.

82 Galatians 3:28.

83 From Jewish Wisdom Literature—Ecclesiasticus 42:13.

84 1 Corinthians 11:5.

85 1 Corinthians 11.

86 Galatians 3:28.

87 Ephesians 5:21–24.

88 Those who taught that you had to become a Jew first before becoming a Christian.

89 Galatians 5:1.

90 Galatians 5:13.

91 Galatians 5:14.

92 Galatians 5:22.

93 2 Corinthians 12:7.

94 Nowadays we might use the expression 'a pain in the neck'. This is the sense in which 'a thorn in my side' would have been used by Paul.

95 Judges 2:3.

96 2 Corinthians 11:26–27.

97   Acts 27 and 28.

98   Acts 23:11.

99   They probably got ashore at what is known as St Paul's Bay today. It ties in with the description of the site of Paul's shipwreck in Acts 27:39–41. A very shallow sandbank runs out and this is probably where the ship struck and began breaking up.

100 1 Corinthians 7:8–9.

101 Genesis 2:24.

102 Romans 12:4–5.

103 Galatians 3:27–28.

104 Colossians 3:14.

105 Ephesians 3:14–19.

★★★ Also by Mike Coles ★★★

THE BIBLE IN COCKNEY
Well, bits of it, anyway

Would you Adam and Eve it? Read how Jesus feeds five thousand geezers with just five loaves of Uncle Fred and two Lilian Gish. Or how Noah built a bloomin' massive nanny. A very down-to-earth 'translation' that brings scripture out of the pulpit and back on to the streets.
ISBN 1 84101 217 3 £5.99

MORE BIBLE IN COCKNEY
Prophets, proverbs and pioneers

Take a butcher's at some of the prophets, proverbs and psalms as well as the Ding-Dong of Ding-Dongs (Song of Songs). To finish off, there is a complete translation of the Captain Hook (book) of Acts into Cockney.
ISBN 1 84101 259 9 £6.99

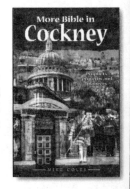

Available from your local bookshop or direct from BRF:
Tel: 01865 319700; e-mail enquiries@brf.org.uk
or visit our website: www.brf.org.uk